PRACTICE! PRACTICE!

A **LATIN VIA OVID** Workbook

Revised Edition

Norma Goldman

Michael Rossi

Wayne State University Press   Detroit

15 14 13 12 11   12 11 10 9 8

_____

ISBN 978-0-8143-2611-4

_____

PREFACE

Practice! Practice! That is the advice given by the native New Yorker to the man who asked how to get to Carnegie Hall. And practice is the way to master the principles of grammar in acquiring a new language, the way to acquire the skills necessary to read Latin with the ease that will make a chore into a pleasure.

Thus the Workbook provides those extra exercises that will give drills in the grammatical concepts for each of the forty chapters of Latin via Ovid. It is assumed that the student has already studied the vocabulary of each lesson, and that he is fairly familiar with the principles of its grammar. He need not have mastered the entire lesson, for that mastery is what the exercises are designed to provide. If the student has not learned the vocabulary items, these exercises will serve also as a reinforcement of the words in the lesson. Whatever forms are needed for the drill are given in the review drills at the beginning of each set of exercises. There is a key in the back of the Workbook so that the student can check his answers, and there are sample quizzes at the end of each body of material. If the student spends the extra time reviewing the principles that emerge from accomplishing these drills and sentence pattern exercises, he will find that the reading becomes clear and the complexity becomes simplified.

The exercises also contain some new directions for practice worked out by innovative teachers who have used the book throughout the country. We are particularly indebted to Ed Phinney of the University of Massachusetts at Amherst for his contributions from the use of the book at the Tufts Institute during the summer. We are also indebted to the following skilled teachers who have contributed supplementary materials: Giovanna Burk of East Lansing High School, Michigan, and Maura Reynolds of Hope College in Holland, Michigan. Michael Rossi of Catholic Central High School in Redford, Michigan, has contributed many of his formulas for exercises and examinations. He has also aided in the preparation of this revised edition, which will tie more closely the Workbook to the Latin via Ovid text, correlating the exercises to each chapter. His expertise from having used the text for the past seventeen years since its first publication with his Latin classes both at Catholic Central and at times at Wayne State University have given him a firsthand familiarity with the needs of students using the text.

We dedicate the book to the students who have worked to help it become a key to unlocking the door beyond which is the pleasurable acquisition of Latin.

Norma Goldman
    Wayne State University

Michael Rossi
    Catholic Central High School

TABLE OF CONTENTS

Chapter I

I. **Fill in** the blanks with the following **case endings**:

(see <u>Latin via Ovid</u>, henceforth <u>LvO</u>, 4)

	Singular	Plural
Nominative	terr____	terr____
Accusative	terr____	terr____
Ablative	terr____	terr____

II. **Change** the following nouns (and their adjectives) to **plural**:

1. puellam
2. rēgīnā
3. charta
4. paenīnsulam
5. terrā pulchrā

6. bonam fābulam
7. parvam īnsulam
8. rēgīnā pulchrā
9. in fābulā prīmā
10. bona terra

Adjectives of size and the adjective <u>bonus</u> often precede their nouns.

III. **Change** these **singular** verbs to **plural** and **translate**:

1. habitat _____ _____
2. rēgnat _____ _____

3. est _____ _____
4. spectat _____ _____

IV. **Change** these **plural** verbs to **singular** and **translate**:

1. rēgnant _____ _____
2. sunt _____ _____

3. habitant _____ _____
4. spectant _____ _____

V. **Translate** the following sentences **into English**:

1. Bonae rēgīnae magnās terrās rēgnant.
2. Puellae pulchrae in parvīs īnsulīs habitant.
3. Ubi sunt magnae īnsulae?
4. In chartā, īnsulae sunt magnae, sed paenīnsulae sunt parvae.
5. Magnās terrās pulchrās rēgnant.
6. Eurōpa in Phoenīcā habitat.
7. Dīdō est rēgīna in terrā Āfricā.
8. Dīdō in Āfricā habitat et rēgnat.

900

2

VI. **Answer** these questions in **complete Latin sentences**:

1. Estne charta magna?

2. Suntne terrae parvae?

3. Ubi sunt terrae?

4. Ubi est Hispānia?

5. Ubi est Ītalia?

6. Ubi est Sicilia?

7. Estne Graecia in Eurōpā?

8. Ubi est Carthāgō?

9. Habitatne Dīdō in Eurōpā?

10. Estne Āfrica terra parva?

VII. **Make up** four sentences of your own from these words:

Subjects	Direct Objects	Verbs
Rēgīna	terrās	spectat
Puella	īnsulam	amat (loves, likes)
Rēgīnae	fābulās	spectant
Puellae	fābulam	amant
Eurōpā	terram	rēgnant

1. _____

2. _____

3. _____

4. _____

Chapter II

I. A. The **genitive case** in Latin is used to show _____.

B. In English the **apostrophe** makes the noun **possessive**:

<u>Singular</u>   (see <u>**LvO**</u>, 14-15) <u>Plural</u>

e.g. the boy's home   e.g. the boys' home

the girl__   the girls__ home

C. Express the same idea by **prepositional phrases**: the home

of the_____ of the_____; of the_____ of the_____

D. The Latin noun <u>puella</u> shows possession by **endings**:

puell_____(s.) of the girl   puell_____(pl.) of the girls

rēgin_____(s.) of the queen   rēgin_____(pl.) of the queens

II. **Change** these words or phrases from **singular** to **plural** in the same case (for nouns) and the same person (for verbs):

e.g. 1. bonam fīliam >bonās fīliās   10. bonam rēginam

2. puellae timidae (gen.)   11. habitat

3. cum bonā amīcā   12. magna terra

4. in parvā īnsulā   13. ad terram novam

5. est   14. portat

6. dē rēginā novā   15. bonum poētam*

7. narrat   16. fugitat

8. amīca timida   17. cum rēginā pulchrā

9. ad paenīnsulam pulchram   18. magnae chartae

*A male poet; a lady poet would be <u>bonam poētam</u> (acc. case).

III. **Translate** these sentences **into English**:

1. Amīcae magnās chartās in terram novam portant.

2. Amīcae rēgīnae ad īnsulam pulchram cum puellīs timidīs fugitant.

3. Poētae fābulās dē īnsulā narrant.

4. Ubi sunt fīliae poētae?

5. Amīca poētae nōn est bona.

6. Puellae fīliās rēgīnae spectant.

7. Amīcae rēgīnae parvās īnsulās spectant.

8. Fīliae rēgīnae cum puellīs timidīs fugitant.

9. Quis (Who) est rēgīna īnsulārum?

4

IV. **Answer** these questions **in Latin**. Write in **complete sentences**:

(Try not to translate but to think in Latin as you reply.)

1. Ubi habitat Eurōpa?

2. Ubi est Tyrus?

3. Quis est taurus?

4. Quis est rēx Phoenīcius?

5. Estne Agēnor taurus?

6. Suntne amīcae Eurōpae timidae?

7. Quis in Olympō habitat?

8. Amatne Eurōpa amīcās?

9. Ubi taurus cum Eurōpā fugitat?

10. Amatne deus Iūppiter Eurōpam?

V. **Word Order**: The normal order of ideas in a Latin sentence is as follows:

SUBJECT   DIRECT OBJECT   PREPOSITIONAL PHRASE   VERB.

Make up five sentences using these words from the categories given. You do not have to have all of the elements in each sentence. This normal word order may vary, depending on what idea is being stressed.

Subject	Direct Object	Prepositional Phrase	Verb
(Noun)	(Noun)	(Preposition + Noun)	
Dīdō	īnsulam	in īnsulā	rēgnat
Eurōpa	terram	in Phoenīcā	habitat
puella	Āfricam	cum amīcīs	spectat
rēgīna	Asiam	in terram pulchram	portat
deus	puellam	in īnsulam	dēsīderat

VI. **Adverbs** and **conjunctions**: These small words keep you from being able to translate fluently. LEARN THEM NOW! **Match** them:

___hic; ___ ita; ___ olim; ___ paene; ___ sed; ___ diu; ____ nunc

1.once; 2.but; 3.for a long time; 4.now; 5.here; 6.thus; 7.almost

Chapter III

I. **Change** these **singular** words or phrases to **plural**:

1. bona dea _____

2. parvā casā _____

3. incola timida _____

4. magistram perītam _____

5. nymphae pulchrae (<u>dat</u>.)_____

6. magnae pictūrae (<u>gen</u>.)_____

7. in magnā silvā _____

8. puella superba _____

9. bona vita _____

10. cum nymphā perītā _____

11. spectat _____

12. labōrat _____

13. rēgnat _____

14. est _____

15. habitat _____

16. amat _____

17. docet _____

18. salvē _____

19. valē _____

20. dat _____

II. **Translate** these sentences **into English**:

1. Dea fābulam narrat.
2. Sapientia agricolae est magna.
3. In magnā silvā habitant agricola et poēta.
4. Dum agricola labōrat, fīlia pictūrās pulchrās fōrmat.
5. Quod discipulae bene labōrant, discipulās magistra amat.
6. Fābulam dē deīs poēta agricolae narrat.

III. **Answer** these questions **in Latin**. Do not translate:

    1. Quis est Minerva?

    2. Quis est Arachnē?

    3. Estne Arachnē dea?

    4. Habitatne dea in terrā?

    5. Cūr (<u>Why</u>) est puella perīta?

    6. Ubi habitant nymphae?

    7. Laudantne nymphae pictūrās puellae?

    8. Suntne pictūrae puellae pulchrae?

    9. Cūr sunt pictūrae puellae pulchrae?

    10. Estne superbia perīculōsa?

IV. **Complete** the marking of the **parts of speech** for each word in the story below (abbreviations listed at bottom of page):

          n   v   n   prep adj   n prep n conj v pro

e.g. Jupiter abducted Europa from her home in Tyre and took her

      adv prep art n   prep n

    swiftly to the island of Crete.   The offspring of this

                        pro

    union was Minos, who gave his name to the kings of Crete.

ABBREVIATIONS FOR PARTS OF SPEECH (See <u>LvO</u>, 418)

n = noun	v = verb	conj = conjunction
pro = pronoun	adv = adverb	int = interjection
adj = adjective (art = article:a,an,the)		prep = preposition

Chapter IV

I. **Complete** the **conjugations** of <u>spectō</u> and <u>respondeō</u> **(see <u>LvO</u>, 30)** in the **present tense**:

spectō, spectāre   respondeō, respondēre

<u>Singular</u>

_____   _____

_____   _____

_____   _____

<u>Plural</u>

_____   _____

_____   _____

_____   _____

II. **Change** these forms from **plural** to **singular (see <u>LVO</u>, 30)** in the same person, and **translate** the **singular** form:

e.g. 1. sunt   est, <u>he/she/it is</u>   11. habētis habēs, <u>you have</u>

e.g. 2. mōnstrāmus mōnstrō, <u>I show</u>   12. clāmant

3. ambulātis   13. sumus

4. negāte!   14. salvēte

5. dēbent   15. fōrmātis

6. docēmus   16. dēsīderāmus

7. estis   17. rēgnāte bene!

8. vocāmus   18. portant

9. simulāte!   19. narrātis

10. certant   20. respondent

III. **Translate** the following **into Latin**:

1. you (pl.) are   6. is she?

2. we are   7. he does deny

3. to be   8. to deny

4. I am   9. they are denying

5. it is   10. are you denying?

8

IV. **Decide** which of these sentences would use the **dative indirect object (see <u>LvO</u>, 30-1)** and which would use **ad + the accusative case** showing **place to which**; then **fill in** the correct forms:

1. The goddess gives the picture to the woman.

   Dea _____ pictūram dat.

2. The teacher gives experience to the students.

   Magistra experientiam _____ dat.

3. The nymphs are carrying the loom to the house.

   Nymphae tēlam ____ _____ portant.

4. The mistress gives a name to her daughter.

   Domina nōmen _____ dat.

5. Minerva does not give wool to the inhabitants of Lydia.

   Minerva lānam _____ Lydiae nōn dat.

6. The king is carrying the map to the island.

   Rēx chartam ____ _____ portat.

7. The poet is telling his story to the women.

   Poēta fābulam _____ nārrat.

8. Give me the book, please.

   Dā librum _____, quaesō.

9. My friend is walking to the woods.

   Meus amīcus ____ _____ ambulat.

10. The farmers are walking to the good land in Africa.

    Agricolae ____ _____ _____ in Āfricā ambulant.

Notice that all the sentences using the **dative case for indirect object** have the idea of **giving, telling, or showing** something to someone; note that the sentences using **ad + the accusative** have an action verb of **carrying, moving, or walking** to a place.

V. **Translate** the following sentences using **complementary infinitives (see LvO, 29)**
   into English:

1. Magistram perītam amāre dēbēmus.

2. Discipulōs magister docēre temptat.

3. Fēminae timidae in silvam fugitāre temptant.

4. Domina agricolīs pictūram dare dēsīderat.

5. Dum in silvīs ambulātis, labōrāre temptō.

6. Dea discipulīs sapientiam dare dēbet.

7. Agricolae casam meam mōnstrāre dēbēs.

8. Agricolīs sapientiam iterum dare temptāmus.

9. Cum magistrā stultā esse nōn dēsīderō.

VI. **Change** these **imperative commands (see LvO, 31)** to **plural**, and **translate**:

e.g. 1. Spectā!   Spectāte!   Look!

   2. Respondē!   _____   _____

   3. Clāmā!   _____   _____

   4. Da!   _____   _____

   5. Labōrā!   _____   _____

   6. Docē!   _____   _____

   7. Laudā!   _____   _____

   8. Salvē!   _____   _____

   9. Valē!   _____   _____

   10. Certā!   _____   _____

VII. **Form** the **stem (see LvO, 29)** from each of these **infinitives**:

   amāre   ambulāre   respondēre   docēre

Chapter V

I. **Change** each of the following to the **imperfect tense (see <u>LvO</u>, 39)**

in the same person and **translate** each **imperfect** form:

e.g 1. vocāmus   vocābāmus   we called, were calling, did call, used to call

   2. docet

   3. mūtat

   4. prohibeō

   5. necātis

   6. pendent

   7. amās

   8. clāmāmus

   9. habitat

   10. portātis

II. **Translate into English**:   **Translate into Latin**:

   (see <u>LvO</u>, 40)

   1. erās _____   7. we were _____

   2. erātis _____   8. they were _____

   3. erat _____   9. you (sing.) were _____

   4. eram _____   10. you (pl.) were _____

   5. erāmus _____   11. I was _____

   6. erant _____   12. she was _____

III. **Fill in** the correct form of the **dative case (see LvO, 30-31, 40)**:

   1. Magistra _____ fābulam narrābat.   (to the girl)

   2. Arachnē pictūrās _____ monstrābat. (to the nymphs)

   3. _____ nōmen est Marcus.   (My, lit. to me)

   4. Sapientia est _____. (yours, s., lit. to you, s.)

   5. Dea pictūrās _____ Lydiae dat. (to the inhabitants)

IV. A. **Commands** are given in a different tone of voice than the
tone used in normal sentences. Statements or questions are
in the **indicative mood**. **Commands** are in the **imperative mood**
(see **LvO**, 31). **Translate** these commands **into English**.
(Remember that each one is in the _____ mood).

1. Spectāte!   2. Clāmāte!   3. Salvēte!   4. Valēte!   5. Docēte!

_____   _____   _____   _____   _____

Now make each **imperative singular**:

_____   _____   _____   _____   _____

B. If you add a person or persons whom you are addressing in a command,
they are put in the **vocative case** (see **LvO**, 31). **Fill in** the **vocative**
of the person addressed in the sentences below. Often the vocative is
postpositive (not the first word in the sentence). Note that in **first
declension nouns** the **vocative and nominative forms are the same**.

1. Spectā, _____, agrōs tuōs.   (farmer)

2. Clāmā, _____, sī (if) auxilium dēsīderās   (mistress)

3. Ō _____, salvē!   (Minerva)

4. Valē, _____; labōrāre nunc dēbeō.   (goddess)

5. Docē, _____, discipulōs bene.   (teacher)

V. Sometimes **vocatives** are used in sentences other than commands.

Fill in the blanks with **vocatives** in these **indicative** sentences:

1. Ō _____, puellam docēre dēbēs.   (Minerva)

2. Deam, _____, vocāre dēbēs.   (Arachne)

3. Sapientiam, _____, habēre dēbētis.   (girls)

4. Pictūrās, _____, spectāre dēbēs.   (mistress)

5. _____, misericordiam habēre dēbēs.   (woman)

6. Ō _____, misericordiam habēre dēbētis. (nymphs)

7. Misericoridam, _____, habēre dēbētis. (farmers)

8. Misericordiam, _____, habēre dēbētis. (goddesses)

Nationality Game

A man who lives in Italy is an Italian in English; in Latin: <u>Italicus</u>.
A woman who lives in Italy is an Italian in English; in Latin: <u>Italica</u>.
Complete these sentences telling what the **female** equivalent is for
each **masculine** form:

(Compare how we indicate the difference between a male and female
graduate in both English and Latin: <u>alumnus</u>, <u>alumna</u>.)

1. a. Puer in Britanniā habitat. Est Britannicus.
   b. Puella in Britanniā habitat. Est _____.

2. a. Puer in Āfricā habitat. Est Āfricānus.
   b. Puella in Āfricā habitat. Est _____.

3. a. Puer in Germāniā habitat. Est Germānicus.
   b. Puella in Germāniā habitat. Est _____.

4. a. Puer in Graeciā habitat. Est Graecus.
   b. Puella in Graeciā habitat. Est _____.

5. a. Marcus in Ītaliā habitat. Est Ītalicus.
   b. Marcia in Ītaliā habitat. Est _____.

6. a. Gaius in Hispāniā habitat. Est Hispānus (or) Hispānicus.
   b. Gaia in Hispāniā habitat. Est _____(or)_____

The names Gaius and Gaia were used in the Roman wedding ceremony:
The bride would say, "<u>Ubi tū Gaius, ego Gaia</u>." The formula meant
literally, "Where you are Gaius, I am Gaia," the equivalent of
"Where you will be, I will be also," or as in the examples above,
"I am your female equivalent."

Chapter VI

I. In Latin, **count backwards** from twelve:

12 _____	8 _____	4 _____
11 _____	7 _____	3 _____
10 _____	6 _____	2 _____
9 _____	5 _____	1 _____

II. **Complete** the declension of <u>bonus puer</u> and <u>templum sacrum</u>:

	MASCULINE		NEUTER	
	<u>Singular</u>	<u>Plural</u>	<u>Singular</u>	<u>Plural</u>
Nom.	bonus puer	bonī puerī	templum sacrum	templa sacra
Gen.	_____	_____	_____	_____
Dat.	_____	_____	_____	_____
Acc.	_____	_____	_____	_____
Abl.	_____	_____	_____	_____

(N.B.: the NEUTER NOMINATIVE AND ACCUSATIVE ARE THE SAME, both singular and plural.)

III. **Masculine nouns** in the **first** declension must be modified by **masculine adjectives**. **Choose** the correct **adjective** in the following sentences:

1. Pīrāta _____ puerum necat. (īrātus/ īrāta)

   (Pīrāta, -ae, <u>m</u>., <u>pirate</u>)

2. Poëtae _____ fābulās nārrābant. (perītī/ perītae)

3. _____ agricolās in agrō spectō. (Multās/ Multōs)

4. Cum nautā _____ nōn navigō (sail). (temerāriā/ temerāriō)

5. Fābulās poëtārum (<u>m</u>.)_____ laudant. (clārōrum/ clārārum)

IV. **Write** the following numbers in **Roman numerals** (see <u>LvO</u>, 48):

575 _____   783 _____   1995 _____

V. **Give the meaning** of each of these **interrogative words**:

1. Cūr Lātōna erat īrāta?   _____, interrogative adverb

2. Quis est Apollo?   _____, interrogative pronoun

3. Ubi puerī exercent?   _____, interrogative adverb

4. Quid dīxit Niobē?   _____, interrogative pronoun

5. Estne īnsula pulchra?   -ne _____, enclitic, interrogative

VI. These small words slow down your translation, if you do not
know their meanings. They are **adverbs** of time, place, or
manner. **Give the English meaning** for each, and then **compose**
short sentences using the verbs suggested below:

<u>Time</u>		<u>Place</u>		<u>Manner</u>	
diū	_____	hīc	_____	ita	_____
ōlim	_____	hūc	_____	bene	_____
nunc	_____	ibi	_____	certē	_____
saepe	_____			maximē	_____
iterum	_____			minimē	_____
aeternō	_____			optimē	_____
prīmō	_____			melius	_____
deinde	_____			paene	_____
dēnique	_____				

Compose six sentences using the **adverbs** above with the **verbs**
given below:

amō, vocō, habitō, labōrō, habeō, portō

e.g. 1. Saepe puerōs vocō.   4. _____

2. _____   5. _____

3. _____   6. _____

Chapter VII

I. **Decline** the following **nouns** with their **adjectives**:

SINGULAR

<u>Feminine</u>	<u>Masculine</u>	<u>Neuter</u>	
rēgia pulchra	equus meus	verbum benignum	same
_____	_____	_____	
_____	_____	_____	
_____	_____	_____ same
_____	_____	_____	

PLURAL

_____	_____	_____ same
_____	_____	_____
_____	_____	_____
_____	_____	_____ same
_____	_____	_____

II. **Change** each **verb** to **plural** in the same person, and give **one** possible **English translation** for that new form:

e.g. 1. convocābat   convocābant   they were calling together

    2. exerceō

    3. honōrās

    4. iuvābat

    5. lacrimās

    6. stō

    7. rogābat

    8. volābās

    9. circumspectābam

    10. monēbātne

III. **Fill in** the blanks with the **ablative of means** (see <u>LvO</u>, 55):

1. Phoebus filiōs rēgīnae _____ necābat.

      (**by means of** arrows = <u>sagitta, -ae</u>, f.)

2. Niobē vītam ultimae filiae _____ rogābat.

      (**with** tears = <u>lacrima, -ae</u>, f.)

3. Deus Mercurius per aera _____ volābat.

      (**with** wings = <u>āla, -ae, f.</u>)

4. Magister discipulōs _____ docēbat.

      (**by means of** words = <u>verbum, -ī</u>, n.)

5. Niobē _____ _____ circumspectābat.

      (**with** eyes = <u>oculus, -ī</u>, m., proud =<u>superbus, -a, -um</u>)

IV. **Translate** each sentence and its answer:

1. Quot equī sunt in agrō?   Septem.
2. Quot filiae in templō stābant? Quattuor.
3. Quot sagittās habēs? Quīnque.
4. Quot filiōs habēs? Trēs.
5. Quot filiās habes? Trēs.
6. Quot līberōs habēs? Sex.
7. Quot fūnera habēbat Niobē? Quattuordecim.
8. Quot digitōs habēs? Decem.   (<u>digitus, -ī</u>, m. = finger)
9. Quot oculōs habēs? Duōs.
10. Quot deōs habent Rōmanī? Multōs, sed duodecim magnōs deōs.

Chapter VIII

I. Give the **future indicative active (see LvO, 63)** of porto and moneo:

	Singular	Plural	Singular	Plural
1st Per.	portābō	portābimus	monēbō	monēbimus
2nd Per.	portā____	_____	monē_____	_____
3rd Per.	_____	_____	_____	_____

II. Give the **Latin** for these phrases **in the correct case**:

1. of good boys   _____
2. best men (nom.)   _____
3. no help (acc.)   _____
4. on a shady bank   in _____
5. of the level field   _____
6. many waves (acc.)   _____
7. wretched men (voc.)   _____
8. of my arms   _____
9. the last sound (nom.) _____
10. to the best man   _____

III. Change these **nominative** phrases to **accusative**, in the **same number** as given:

e.g. 1. puerī miserī   puerōs miserōs
    2. auxilium nullum   _____
    3. bracchium tuum   _____
    4. concilia digna   _____
    5. fuga ultima   _____
    6. papȳrī densī   _____
    7. satyrus miser   _____
    8. sonus nullus   _____
    9. virī cēterī   _____
   10. dī (deī) magnī   _____

IV. **Change** the verb in each sentence to the **future tense (see <u>LvO</u>, 63)**

and **translate** the new sentence:

1. Pān Syringam vocat.

    <u>vocābit.</u>   Pan will call Syrinx.

2. Syringa satyrum videt.

   _____   _____

3. Satyrī nymphās amant.

   _____   _____

4. Nympha trāns agrōs fugitat.

   _____   _____

5. Nymphae Syringam trānsfōrmant.

   _____   _____

6. Auxilium nullum habeō.

   _____   _____

7. Bonōs agrōs nōn habēmus.

   _____   _____

8. Estne sonus magnus?

   _____   _____

9. Habēsne verba nulla?

   _____   _____

10. Lacrimās nōn habeō.

   _____   _____

V. **Answer** aloud these questions in **complete Latin sentences:**

1. Amābitne Pān Syringam aeternō?

2. Dēvovēbitne sē Syringa Diānae?

3. Habēbitne nullus vir, nullus deus Syringam?

4. Quid Pān in bracchiīs tenēbit?

5. Quae (<u>who, f. pl.</u>) Syringam in papyrōs trānsfōrmābunt?

VI. **Translate** the following verbs **into English:**

1. erunt _____ eritis _____

2. erimus _____ eris _____

3. erō _____ erit _____

Chapter IX

I. **Conjugate** in the **perfect tense (see LvO, 71)** the following verbs:

portō, -āre, -āvī, -ātum   doceō, -ēre, docuī, doctum

<u>portāvī</u>   I have carried, carried*   <u>docuī</u>   I have taught, taught*

_____ _____   _____ _____

_____ _____   _____ _____

_____ _____   _____ _____

_____ _____   _____ _____

_____ _____   _____ _____

*The English "did carry, did teach" are necessary for emphasis and questions.

II. **Give** the **perfect** or the **imperfect** forms **(see <u>LvO</u>, 71-72)** for the

following verbs:

e.g. 1. he has seen   1. vīdit

2. we have told   2. _____

3. they were telling   3. _____

4. you (s.) have loved   4. _____

5. she was calling   5. _____

6. you (pl.) have given   6. _____

7. I have stood   7. _____

8. I used to stand   8. _____

9. Have they helped?   9. _____?

10. we have had   10. _____

III. **Fill in** the blanks with the **dative** form that will complete the

idea of the **adjective (see <u>LvO</u>, 73)** in the following sentences:

1. Arcadia est terra _____ cāra.   (to the god)

2. Arcadiam, terram _____ cāram vīdī.   (to the god)

3. Callisto erat _____ grāta.   (to the god)

4. Nympham _____ grātam vīdī.   (to the god)

5. Verba tua nōn sunt _____ grāta.   (to me)

6. Erat persōna _____ nōn grāta.   (to Italy)

(<u>persōna</u> = a person)

IV. **Use** the correct form of the **future tense** to complete both
clauses **(see LvO, 73)** in these **conditional** sentences:

1. Sī dea mē _____, īrāta _____.

           (will see, sees)   (she will be)

2. Sī nōs linguam Latīnam _____, laetī _____.

                (you will teach, teach)   (we will be)

3. Sī in herbā_____, stellās in caelo _____.

          (I shall lie, lie)   (I shall see)

4. Sī deōs _____, _____.

    (I shall call upon, call upon)   (they will reply)

5. Sī agrōs _____, agrī pretium bonum _____.

     (you will take care of, take care of)   (they will give)

6. Sī vestīmenta _____, pulchra _____.

   (we will take care of, take care of)   (they will be)

7. Sī vītam suam _____, vīta pretium bonum _____.

   (he will take care of, takes care of)   (it will give)

V. **Choose** the correct form of the **adjective suus, -a, um** or the
pronoun eius. Remember that suus -- his, her, its, their own --
must refer to the **subject** of the sentence. Then **translate** each
sentence.

1. Parentēs (parents) fīliōs _____ amāre dēbent   (their)

2. Marcus vestīmenta _____ nōn amat.   (her)

3. Fibula vestīmenta _____ rētinēbat.   (her)

4. Dominae vestīmenta _____ fibulīs rētinēbant.   (their)

5. Arcas mātrem _____ paene necāvit.   (his)

6. Arachnē pictūrās _____ nōn amābat (her = Minerva's)

7. Arachnē pictūrās _____ amābat.   (her own)

VI. What is your **Zodiac (see LvO, 77)** sign? What does it mean?

Chapter X

I. Conjugate the following verbs in the **perfect indicative (see LvO, 81):**

dō, dare, dedī, datum   videō, vidēre, vīdī, vīsum

<u>dedī</u>   I have given, I gave*   <u>vīdī</u>   I have seen, I saw*

<u>dedistī</u> _____   <u>vīdistī</u> _____

_____ _____   _____ _____

_____ _____   _____ _____

_____ _____   _____ _____

_____ _____   _____ _____

*The English "did give, did see" are necessary for emphasis and questions.

II. Translate the following verbs in a form that clearly indicates the tense. **Translate 1-4 into English; translate 5-8 into Latin:**

1. mansērunt _____   5. he has been present _____

2. servāvistī _____   6. I have fled _____

3. tetendī _____   7. we were awaiting _____

4. portāvimus _____   8. we have awaited _____

III. Choose the correct form of the **two verbs** given below:

1. We have given gifts to the sons of the queen.

   Dona filiīs rēgīnae _____.   (dabāmus/ dedimus)

2. The animals were standing in the forest.

   Animālia in silvā _____.   (stābant/ stetērunt)

3. Arcas was trying to kill the bear with a javelin.

   Arcas ursam iaculō necāre _____. (temptābat/ tempāvit)

4. No words have remained in the nymph.

   Nulla verba in nymphā _____. (manēbant/ mansērunt)

IV. A. **Fill in** the missing **principal parts (see LvO, 80)** for the

   following verbs, and give the English meaning:

1st Per. Sing. Pres.	Infinitive	1st Per. Sing. Perf.	P.P.Part.	English
1. videō	_____	vīdī	vīsum	see
2. maneō	manēre	_____	XXXXX	remain
3. portō	portāre	_____	portātum	carry
4. _____	abesse	āfuī	āfutūrum	be absent
5. adsum	_____	adfuī	adfutūrum	be present
6. exspectō	exspectāre	_____	exspectātum	await
7. dō	dare	_____	datum	give
8. stō	_____	stetī	statum	stand
9. habeō	_____	habuī	habitum	have
10. iuvō	iuvāre	_____	iūtum	aid, help

1B. Why is it important to know the **infinitive**?_____

C. Why is it important to know the **third principal part**?_____

V. **Give the Latin** for the following **numbers (see LvO, 81; 426-27)**:

1. 6 + 7 = 13   Sex et septem fiunt _____.

2. 8 + 8 = 16   Octo et octo fiunt _____.

3. 19 - 4 = 15   Undēvīgintī minus quattuor fiunt _____.

VI. **Give the perfect tense (see LvO, 82)** of sum, esse, fuī, futūrum, :

fuī, _____, _____, _____, _____, _____

Chapter XI

I. A. **Complete the declension** of <u>alma</u> (kind, nourishing) <u>māter</u>, an **adjective of the first declension** modifying a **third declension noun**:

	Singular	Plural
Nom.	alma māter	_____
Gen.	_____	_____
Dat.	_____	_____
Acc.	_____	_____
Abl.	_____	_____

B. What is an <u>alma māter</u>? _____

II. The word <u>rēx</u>, <u>rēgis</u>, m. (king) is the basis for many words associated with kings, royalty, and ruling. Note that they are almost all formed from the **genitive case singular**, evidence that the genitive is very important and must be learned with each noun.

Complete the **Latin** words that are associated with this <u>reg-</u> base in the first column, and the **English** words in the second **(see <u>LvO</u>, 95)**:

Latin		English	
rēg_____	a palace	reg_____	royal
rēg_____	to rule	reg_____	one who kills a king
rēg_____	queen	Elizabeth Reg_____	Queen Elizabeth

III. <u>Mille</u> **(see <u>LvO</u>, 89)** is a Latin word with many English cognates.

A. What does <u>mille</u> mean in Latin? _____

B. Give two English words based on this root:_____ &_____

C. What is a "mill" in taxation language? _____

D. What is the plural of <u>mille</u>? _____

E. What English word meaning "thousands of feet" (<u>mīlia</u> <u>passuum</u>) is derived from this plural form? _____

IV. Third declension nouns <u>finis, finis</u>, m. and <u>pars, partis</u>, f.

  A. In what case are these nouns different from others in this

    declension?_____

  B. **Give** the **genitive plural** of each: _____ and _____

  C. What are these nouns called? _____ of the 3rd declension

V. **Change** these **singular** phrases to **plural** in the **same case**:

    1. pars ultima   (nom.)   _____

    2. patris nostrī   (gen.)   _____

    3. bonō rēgī   (dat.)   _____

    4. piscem immensum (acc.)   _____

    5. senis piī   (gen.)   ____senum_____

    6. membrum longum (acc.)   _____

    7. mensā planā   (abl.)   _____

    8. arbor umbrōsa   (nom.)   _____

    9. dominō benignō (dat.)   _____

   10. servō miserō   (dat.)   _____

VI. <u>Duo et duae et duo fiunt sex</u>. **Fill in** the correct form of <u>duo</u>

   (see <u>LvO</u>, 89, 423):

    1. Two queens cannot live in one palace.

       _____ rēgīnae in ūnā rēgiā habitāre nōn possunt.

    2. The daughters of the two queens are pretty.

      Fīliae _____ rēgīnārum sunt pulchrae.

    3. We have given presents to the two queens.

      Dōna _____ rēgīnīs dedimus.

    4. I have watched the two queens in their palaces.

      _____ rēgīnās in rēgiīs eārum spectāvī.

    5. A king does not live with two queens.

      Rēx cum _____ rēgīnīs nōn habitat.

    6. A queen cannot love two kings.

      Rēgīna _____ rēgēs amāre nōn potest.

Chapter XII

I. **Complete** the singular and plural **declension** for <u>nōmen fāmōsum</u>:

> **(see <u>LvO</u>, 92)**

	Singular		Plural	
Nom.	nōmen fāmōsum	same	nōmina fāmōsa	same
Gen.	_____		_____	
Dat.	_____		_____	
Acc.	_____	same	_____	same
Abl.	_____		_____	

Note that the **nominative and accusative, singular and plural are the same** in each case, and that **both neuter plurals end in -<u>a</u>**.

II. **Fill in** the blanks after <u>video</u> with an **infinitive** whose
subject is in the accusative case (see <u>LvO</u>, 99).

e.g. 1. I see that the boys are living well.

> Videō puerōs bene <u>vīvere</u>.

2. I see that the slaves are stretching out their arms.

> Videō serv____ bracchia _____.

3. I see that the mothers tell stories about their daughters.

> Videō mātr____ fābulās dē fīliābus _____.

4. I see that the old folks are catching the goose.

> Videō sen____ anserem _____.

5. I see that men are living very well.

> Videō homin____ optimē _____.

Consult the **English-Latin Vocabulary** in <u>LvO</u>, <u>479-87</u>, for needed words.

III. **Choose** the correct form of the two given in parentheses for

the **adjective used as a noun, a substantive (see LvO, 100)**:

1. I do not like evil men.   (Malōs/ Mala) nōn amō.

2. I want good things.   (Bonōs/ Bona) dēsīderō.

3. We fear many men.   (Multōs/ Multa) timēmus.

4. We fear many things.   (Multōs/ Multa) timēmus.

5. Pious men ought not to fear   (Piī/ Piōs) deōs nōn timēre

        the gods.   dēbent.

IV. **Give** the **principal parts** and meaning for each of the following verbs

and **indicate** to **which conjugation** each belongs:

e.g 1. vastō   vastāre (1)   vastāvī   vastātum   destroy

2. vīvō _____ _____ _____ _____

3. timeō _____ _____ XXXXXX _____

4. dubitō _____ _____ _____ _____

5. iubeō _____ _____ _____ _____

6. parō _____ _____ _____ _____

7. sedeō _____ _____ _____ _____

V. **Change** the above verbs into **negative commands, both singular**

and **plural (see LvO, 99-100)**:

<u>Singular</u>   <u>Plural</u>

e.g 1. Nōlī terrās vastāre.   Nōlīte terrās vastāre.

2. _____ male vīvere.   _____.

3. _____ deōs t_____.   _____.

4. _____ deōs d_____.   _____.

5. _____ puerōs i_____.   _____.

6. _____ cēnam p_____.   _____.

7. _____ in templō s_____.   _____.

VI. **Give** the **past perfect** for each of the above verbs in the **3rd person**

singular: e.g. <u>vastāverat</u>; <u>vīxerat</u>; <u>etc.</u>

Chapter XIII

I. **Complete the declension** of <u>nox clārissima</u>, the clearest night:

(see <u>LvO</u>, 107)

	<u>Singular</u>	<u>Plural</u>
Nom.	nox clārissima	_____
Gen.	_____	_____
Dat.	_____	_____
Acc.	_____	_____
Abl.	_____	_____

(N.B.: <u>nox, noctis</u>, f. is a 3rd declension I-stem noun)

II. **Give the superlative** for the **adjectives** in these phrases:

1. flōs _____ (grātus, -a, -um)

2. flūmen _____ (nōtus, -a, -um)

3. fons _____ (clārus, -a, -um)

4. imāgō _____ (grātus, -a, -um)

5. iuvenis _____ (fōrmōsus, -a, -um)

6. mōns _____ (altus, -a, -um)

7. potestās _____ (magnus, -a, -um > maximus, -a, -um)

8. vox _____ (raucus, -a, -um)

9. soror _____ (cārus, -a, -um)

10. corpus _____ (fōrmōsus, -a, -um)

III. **Conjugate** <u>amō, -āre, -āvī, -ātum</u> and <u>iubeō, -ēre, iussī, iussum</u>

in the **future perfect tense** (see <u>LvO</u>, 109):

amāverō	I shall have loved	iusserō	I shall have ordered
_____	you will have loved	_____	you will have ordered
_____	she will have loved	_____	he will have ordered
_____	we shall have loved	_____	we shall have ordered
_____	you will have loved	_____	you will have ordered
_____	they will have loved	_____	they will have ordered

IV. **Fill in** the blanks with the correct form of <u>posse</u> **(see <u>LvO</u>, 108)**:

1. Putāre _____.   I can think.

2. Reportāre _____.   We are able to report.

3. Id dēvorāre _____.   He is able to devour it.

4. Mē humāre _____.   You (pl.) can bury me.

5. Sibi nocēre _____.   She can harm herself.

6. Parāre _____.   You (sing.) can prepare.

7. Tē tangere _____.   I can touch you.

8. Pervidēre _____.   They can discern.

9. Dēsistere nōn _____.   He cannot stop.

10. Mē turbāre nōn _____.   It cannot disturb me.

V. **Fill in** the blanks with the correct **ablative case (see <u>LvO</u>, 108)**:

1. Echo had harmed Juno by means of a trick. (trick, <u>dolus</u>, -ī, m.)

    Echo Iūnōnī _____ nocuerat.

2. The table was made level with a piece of a broken pot. (piece of

    broken pot = <u>testa</u>, -<u>ae</u>, f.)

    Mensa _____ plāna facta est.

3. Mercury was walking on earth with Jupiter. (<u>Iuppiter, Iovis</u>, m.)

    Mercurius cum _____ in terrā ambulābat.

4. The flower with white petals (petal, <u>folium</u>, -<u>iī</u>, n.)

         was called Narcissus.

    Flōs _____ _____ Narcissus appellātus est.

VI. A. **Translate** each <u>quem</u> **(interrogative pronoun)** question

     (see <u>LvO</u>, 153):

1. Quem Echo amāvit?

2. Quem Iuppiter servāvit?

3. Quem Arachnē vocāvit?

B. **Translate** each sentence **(relative pronoun, see <u>LvO</u>, 143)**:

1. Iuvenis quem Echo amāvit erat Narcissus.

2. Iuvenis quem Iuppiter servāvit erat Arcas.

3. Dea quam Arachnē vocāvit erat Minerva.

Chapter XIV

I. **Conjugate** the 3rd declension verb dūcō, -ere, dūxī, ductum in
the tenses indicated **(see LvO, 117-18)**:

Present	Imperfect	Perfect	Pluperf.	Fut. Perf.
1 dūcō	dūcēbam	dūxī	dūxeram	dūxerō
2 _____ _____		_____	_____	_____
3 _____ _____		_____	_____	_____
1 _____ _____		_____	_____	_____
2 _____ _____		_____	_____	_____
3 _____ _____		_____	_____	_____

II. **Conjugate** the 3rd declension-io verb faciō, -ere, fēcī, factum:
(see LvO, 118)

1 faciō	faciēbam	fēcī	fēceram	fēcerō
2 _____ _____		_____	_____	_____
3 _____ _____		_____	_____	_____
1 _____ _____		_____	_____	_____
2 _____ _____		_____	_____	_____
3 _____ _____		_____	_____	_____

Note the places where the 3rd-io verb differs from the regular 3rd
conjugation verb.

III. The **personal pronouns** are usually not used in the **nominative**
case, unless the **subject** is being emphasized: Ego putō! I
think (so)! **Fill in** the blanks with the correct **personal pronoun**
in the proper case **(see LvO, 119, 423)** and **translate**:

1. _____ tē amō, sed _____ mē nōn amās.   (I)...(you)

2. _____ dōna dedērunt.   (to us)

3. _____ fābulam narrā, quaesō.   (to them)

4. _____ fābulās poētae amāmus.   (we)

5. Dominus _____.   (add cum to the pronoun; with you, pl.)

IV. A. <u>Partēs corporis</u>. **Indicate body parts (see <u>Practice</u>! Key, 118)**

on the drawing:

<u>Masculine</u>	<u>Feminine</u>	<u>Neuter</u>
oculus, -i <u>eye</u>	lingua,-ae <u>tongue</u>	corpus,-oris <u>body</u>
nāsus, -ī <u>nōse</u>	manus,-ūs hand	caput,-itis head
digitus, -ī <u>finger</u>	clāvīcula,-ae clavicle	pectus,-oris chest
collus, -ī <u>neck</u>	tībia, -ae <u>leg bone</u>	ōs, ōris <u>mouth</u>
pēs, pedis <u>foot</u>	vertebra, -ae <u>vertebra</u>	crūs, crūris <u>leg</u>
venter, -tris <u>stomach</u>	vēna, -ae <u>vein</u>	brācchium, -iī <u>limb</u>
capillus, -ī <u>hair</u>	artēria, -ae <u>artery</u>	abdōmen, -inis <u>abdomen</u>
musculus, -ī <u>muscle</u>	faciēs, -eī <u>face</u>	membrum, -ī <u>leg,arm</u>
dens, -ntis <u>tooth</u>	auris, auris <u>ear</u>	cor, cordis <u>heart</u>
tālus, -ī <u>heel</u>	patella, -ae <u>kneecap</u>	cerebrum, -ī <u>cerebrum</u>
truncus, -ī <u>trunk</u>	cauda, -ae <u>tail</u>	supercilium, -ī <u>eyebrow</u>
humerus, -ī <u>shoulder</u>	frons, -ntis <u>forehead</u>	genū, -ūs <u>knee</u>

N.B. Not all of the words can be put into the drawing.

B. **Give** the **Latin roots** of these English words:

1. capital <u>caput, -itis</u>, n.   15. nasal   _____

2. facial   _____   16. dental   _____

3. collar   _____   17. supercilious _____

4. coronary   _____   18. linguist   _____

5. cordial   _____   19. abdominal   _____

6. digit   _____   20. digital   _____

7. abdomen   _____   21. genuflect   _____

8. pedal   _____   22. manual   _____

9. capillary _____   23. pectoral   _____

10. cerebral _____   24. bracchial   _____

11. frontal   _____   25. muscle   _____

12. oculist   _____   26. trunk   _____

13. aural   _____   27. member   _____

14. oral   _____   28. corporal   _____

PARTES CORPORIS

IV. A. PARTES CORPORIS

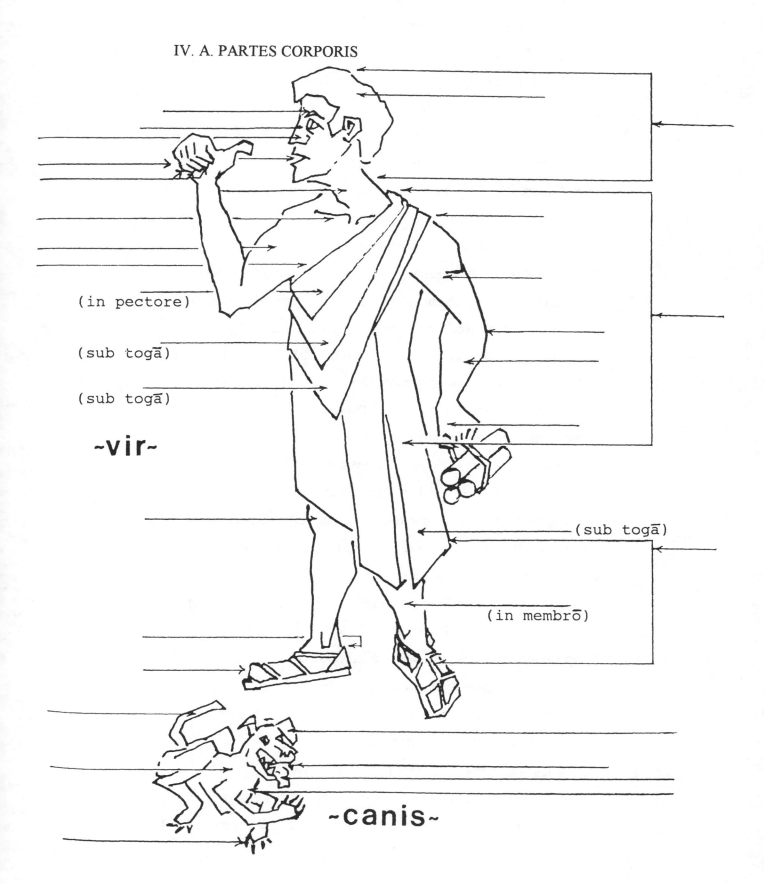

(in pectore)

(sub togā)

(sub togā)

~vir~

(sub togā)

(in membrō)

~canis~

V. **Put the proper endings** on the words below:

1. In corpor_____ hūmānō sunt duo bracchi_____.

2. In bracchi_____ sunt manūs et digitī.

3. Homō decim digit_____ habet.

4. Homō decim digit_____ in ped_____ habet.

5. In capit_____ sunt capill_____.

6. Mīles crūr_____ (pl.) hostis telō vulnerat.

7. Senex ventr_____ magnum habet.

8. Cibum dent_____ mandimus. (mandere = to chew)

9. Ocul_____ vidēmus. (with our eyes)

10. Ped_____ ambulāmus. (with our feet)

VI. A. Sight passage: Menenius Agrippa was sent as ambassador to persuade the plebians (plebs) to return to their homes after they had left Rome in anger at being denied their rights by the patricians (patrici). **Translate into English** the speech of Agrippa:

"Corpus hūmānum multa membra habet inter quae sunt manūs, ōs, dentēs, venter, crūra. Ōlim reliquae (the rest of) partēs corporis īrātae erant quod venter omnia accēpit sed nihil sibi ēgit. Tum inter sē hoc consilium cēpērunt. Dentēs nullum cibum mandere, ōs nullum cibum accipere, manūs nullum cibum ad ōs portāre statuērunt (They agreed that . . .). Itaque tōtum corpus valēre nōn poterat et ē vītā discessit. Nōlīte, cīvēs, propter discordiam vestram eōdem (the same) modō patriam dēlēre (destroy).

"Necesse est corpus hūmānum omnēs partēs habēre; necesse est patriam et patriciōs et plēbem habēre." Plebs fābulam Menēnii Agrippae intellēxit (understood) et condiciōnēs pacis accēpit.*

B. From the information given above, **answer** these questions:

1. Eratne Menēnius Agrippa plēbēius an (or) patricius?

2. Quae sunt quinque partēs corporis?

3. Cūr reliquae partēs erant īrātae contrā ventrem?

4. Estne necesse corpus hūmānum omnēs partēs habēre?

*Adapted from Experimental Materials from U of M Workshop, 1953.

PARTES CORPORIS CROSSWORD PUZZLE

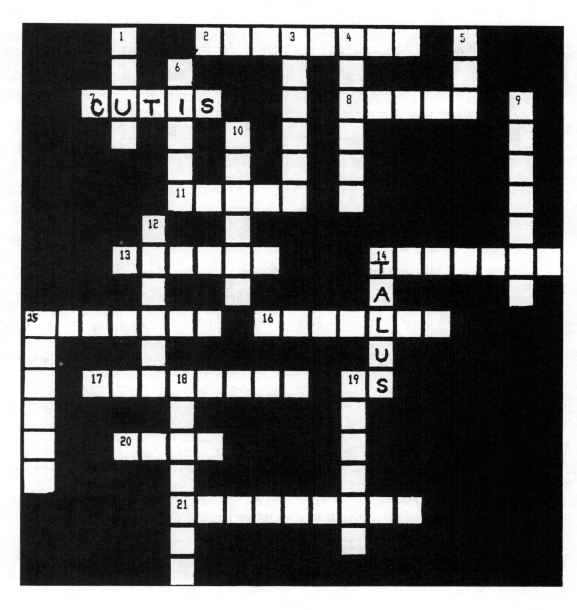

ACROSS
2. Muscle
7. Skin
8. Nose
11. Ear
13. Chest
4. Trunk
15. Finger
16. Hair
17. Backbone
19. Mouth
20. Leg
21. Collarbone

DOWN
1. Leg
3. Neck
4. Tongue
5. Foot
6. Legbone
9. Leg or arm
10. Body
12. Stomach
14. Heel
15. Teeth
18. Torso
19. Eye

Chapter XV

I. Below is a sample verb from each conjugation. **Conjugate** each in the **future tense (see LvO, 126)**:

I	II	III	III-iō	IV
vocābō -bō manēbō		dūcam	capiam	sentiam
_____ _____		_____ _____	_____	_____
_____ _____		_____ _____	_____	_____
_____ -bi- _____		_____ -e- _____ -ie- _____ -ie-		
_____ _____		_____ _____	_____	_____
_____ -bu- _____		_____ _____	_____	_____

II. **Give a synopsis (see LvO, 126)** of the verbs given above, changing the **person** and **number** for each:

	1st S.	2nd S.	3rd S.	1st Pl.	3rd Pl.
Pres.	vocō	manēs	dūcit	capimus	sentiunt
Imp.	_____	_____	_____	_____	_____
Fut.	_____	_____	_____	_____	_____
Perf.	_____	_____	_____	_____	_____
PPerf.	_____	_____	_____	_____	_____
FPerf.	_____	_____	_____	_____	_____

III. In the blanks, **give the superlative** forms for these **adjectives ending in -er (see LvO, 127)**:

1. Clōdia erat puella _____ in terrā.

    (pulcher, -chra, -chrum)

2. Spartacus erat servus _____ in castrīs.

    (miser, -era, -erum)

3. Dī casam senum in templum _____ mūtāvērunt.

    (sacer, -cra, -crum)

35

IV. **Translate** these sentences **into English**:

1. Quamquam virī prope suās casās manēre dēbent, per oppida errant.

2. Sī fīlius tuus iaculum suō manū tenēbit, cēterī līberī eum vidēbunt.

3. Sī auxilium nullum virō dabō, mihi amīcus nōn erit.

4. Mōnstrābisne mihi pretium gladiī secretō?

5. Ubi ad ōrāculī nōtī oppidum appropinquāvī, cūr mē ēvitāvistī?

6. Sī per caelum volābis, tibi auxilium maximum hominēs dabunt.

7. Nōs in oppidō perīculōsō mansimus, sed vōs prope rīpam cēlāvistis.

8. Amantēs consilium habent: parentēs fallent et domūs relinquent
   et ad tumulum Ninī convenient.

9. Pȳramus quoque mortem quaeret si vēlāmina cruenta Thisbēs
   (<u>Greek</u> <u>genitive</u> <u>singular</u>) vidēbit.

V. **Supply** the correct **reflexive pronoun** or **possessive adjective** in
   these sentences (see <u>LvO</u>, 110, 119, 172):

1. Iuppiter in nimbō (in a cloud) _____ cēlāvit.   (himself)

2. Iūnō _____ semper iuvat.   (herself)

3. Deae _____ cūrābunt.   (themselves)

4. Dī _____ nōn fallunt.   (themselves)

5. Iuppiter _____ iuvat.   (her)

6. Iuppiter _____ iuvat.   (them)

7. Iuppiter amīcōs _____ iuvat.   (his own)

8. Iuppiter amīcōs _____ iuvat.   (Mercury's) (his)

9. Iuppiter _____ iuvat.   (me)

10. Fīlius _____ erat Mercurius.   (his)

VI. **Indicate** the **conjugation (1, 2, 3, 3, 3-io, 4)** of each verb below
and the **future tense sign, -bi or -e (-ie-)** (see <u>LvO</u>, 126):

1.	bibō, bibere, bibī, bibitum	drink	3	-ē-
2.	conveniō, -īre, -vēnī, -ventum	meet	4	-iē-
3.	fallō, -ere, fefellī, falsum	deceive	____	____
4.	fugiō, -ere, fūgī, -itum	flee	____	____
5.	optō, -āre, -āvī, -ātum	hope	____	____
6.	perveniō, -īre, -vēnī, -ventum	arrive	____	____
7.	quaerō, -ere, quaesīvī, -sītum	seek	____	____
8.	dēbeo, -ere, dēbuī, -itum	ought, owe	____	____
9.	relinquō, -ere, -līquī, -lictum	leave	____	____
10.	sentiō, -īre, sēnsī, sēnsum	feel	____	____
11.	timeō, -ēre, timuī	fear	____	____
12.	veniō, -īre, vēnī, ventum	come	____	____

VII. **Tell** what **case** each of these **prepositions** governs and **choose**
the correct **noun object** of the two given in parentheses:

ex + _____	ex _____	(oppidum/ oppidō)
sub + _____ or ____	sub _____	(undīs/ undās)
ad + _____	ad _____	(īnsulā/ īnsulam)
in + _____ or ____	in _____	(silvā/ silvam)
dē + _____	dē _____	(pōmā, pōmīs)
ab + _____	ab _____	(itinere/ iter)
prō + _____	prō _____	(domū/ domum)
cum + _____	cum _____	(leōne/ leōnem)
inter + _____	inter _____	(amantēs/ amantibus)
post + _____	post _____	(morte/ mortem)
propter + _____	propter _____	(cruōre/ cruōrem)
trans + _____	trans _____	(pariete, parietem)
per + _____	per _____	(fissō/ fissum)
prope + _____	prope _____	(arbore/ arborem)
praeter + _____	praeter _____	(duce/ ducem)

Chapter XVI

I. **Decline** the **demonstrative pronouns** hic **(this)** and ille **(that)**:

(see LvO, 133)

	Masc.	Fem.	Neut.	Masc.	Fem.	Neut.
			SINGULAR			
N.	hic	haec	hoc	ille	illa	illud
G.	_____	_____	_____	_____	_____	_____
D.	_____	_____	_____	_____	_____	_____
A.	_____	_____	_____	_____	_____	_____
A.	_____	_____	_____	_____	_____	_____

			PLURAL			
N.	_____	_____	_____	_____	_____	_____
G.	_____	_____	_____	_____	_____	_____
D.	_____	_____	_____	_____	_____	_____
A.	_____	_____	_____	_____	_____	_____
A.	_____	_____	_____	_____	_____	_____

II. When hic and ille modify nouns (**this** lion or **that** plan), they
are **demonstrative adjectives** and must agree with the noun they
modify in **case, number, and gender**, but not necessarily in
ending **(see LvO, 133)**. **Fill in** the blanks:

	Masculine	Feminine	Neuter
		SINGULAR	
N.	hic leō	haec hōra	hoc consilium
G.	huius leōnis	huius hōrae	huius consiliī
D.	huic leōnī	huic hōrae	huic consiliō
A.	_____	_____	_____
A.	_____	_____	_____

(**Complete** the plurals on the following page)

PLURAL

N.	hī leōnēs	hae hōrae	haec consilia
G.	_____	_____	_____
D.	_____	_____	_____
A.	_____	_____	_____
A.	_____	_____	_____

III. **Write in Latin** the forms of the **demonstrative adjective** <u>ille</u> (see <u>LvO</u>, 133):

1. of that danger   _____ perīculī

2. that memorial (nom.)   _____ monumentum

3. in those urns   in _____ urnīs

4. of those companions (m.)   _____ comitum

5. to that lover   _____ amantī

6. those apples (acc.)   _____ pōma

7. those times (nom.)   _____ tempora

8. of those swords   _____ gladiōrum

9. by those plans   _____ consiliīs

10. on that journey   in _____ itinere

IV. **Change** these **singular imperatives (see <u>LvO</u>, 134)** to **plural** (note the change in the **possessive adjective**):

1. Amā hostēs tuōs!   _____ hostēs vestrōs.

2. Monē amīcōs tuōs!   _____ amīcōs vestrōs.

3. Pete domum tuam!   _____ domūs vestrās.

4. Cape tēlum tuum!   _____ tēla vestra.

5. Sentī perīculum tuum!   _____ perīculum vestrum.

V. **Give a synopsis** of <u>legō</u>, 1st per. pl. (Note various meanings):

1. Librōs _____.   We read books.

2. Flōrēs _____.   We were picking flowers.

3. Hoc consilium _____.   We shall choose this plan.

4. Litterās _____.   We have read the letter

5. Herbās _____.   We had picked the herbs.

6. Illum consilium _____.   We shall have chosen that plan.

Chapter XVII

I. A. **Give the Enlish equivalent** for each of these **passive endings:**

   (see   **LvO**, 142-43)

SINGULAR		PLURAL	
-r	_____	-mur	_____
-ris	_____	-minī	_____
-tur	_____	-ntur	_____

B. What is the **tense sign** for the **imperfect** in the **passive voice**?

For all conjugations: _____

C. What is the **tense sign** for the **future** in the **passive voice**?

For 1st and 2nd conjugations: _____ ; for 3rd and 4th: _____

II. Using the information above, **give one simple English meaning** for the following **passive** forms:

1. vocor _____
2. monēbāris _____
3. petētur _____
4. facimur _____
5. faciēbāmur _____
6. sentiuntur _____
7. vocāminī _____
8. petēris _____
9. facitur _____
10. monēminī _____

III. **Translate** these **relative pronouns (see LvO, 143-44),** indicating the **case** and **number**, when not clear from the translation:

1. cui _____
2. de quibus _____
3. quōs _____
4. quae _____
5. ad quem _____
6. sine quō _____
7. quibuscum _____
8. cuius _____
9. post quem _____
10. ā quā _____
11. quibus (dat.) _____
12. quod _____
13. propter quod _____
14. quī _____
15. quem _____
16. quās _____
17. quōrum _____
18. per quae _____
19. quārum _____
20. quō _____

IV. **Translate** these sentences **into English**:

1. Hic iuvenis potentiā amōris movētur.

2. Atalanta virgo fugitat amantem quem timet.

3. Vocābam fēminam quae ab illīs damnābātur.

4. Ille ēvītāvit perīculum quod ā nōbīs timēbātur.

5. Pulcherrima dea amōris, quae ab omnibus adōrātur, iuvenem
   iuvābit.

6. Facite illa quae facere dēbētis.

7. Nōn amō hunc hominem quī aliōs nōn amat.

8. Hī rēgem timuērunt cuius oppidum capiēbātur.

9. Illum hominem nesciō cuī auxilium dabātur.

10. Haec pōma quae ā deā dabantur tē iuvābunt.

V. **Fill in** the correct form of the **relative pronoun** (see <u>LvO</u>, 143-44)
   in these sentences:

1. Magistra _____ ā discipulīs amātur est pulcherrima.

   (who)

2. Puerum _____ servābātur ego vīdī.

   (who)

3. Māter _____ fīliī mortuī sunt cūrābitur.

   (whose)

4. Fugite ad parentem _____ vōbīs nōn nocēbit.

   (who)

5. Ignoscet magistra erroribus discipulōrum _____ amat.

   (whom)

6. Homō dē _____ dicēbās ab hostibus capiēbātur.

   (whom)

Chapter XVIII

I. A. In the **perfect passive participle** v̄isus, -a, -um, which means

"(having been) seen" **(see LvO, 151-53)**, which word in the English

meaning indicates that the idea is **perfect**? _____

                        that the idea is **passive**?_____

                        that the idea is a **participle**? _____

B. The **perfect passive participle** is a **verbal** _____

declined like the **adjective** _____, _____, _____

in all the five cases, singular and plural.

C. **Give** the **perfect passive particple** for the following verbs

and the literal English translation:

e.g.1. dūcō   ductus, -a, -um   (having been) led

    2. adōrō   _____   _____

    3. carpō   _____   _____

    4. parō   _____   _____

    5. iaciō   _____   _____

    6. prōmittō_____   _____

    7. scrībō   _____   _____

    8. capiō   _____   _____

II. **Choose** the correct **perfect passive participle** to modify each

noun in the following phrases:

1. virgo _____ (having been) led   (nom. sing.)

2. deam _____ (having been) adored   (acc. sing.)

3. pōma _____ (having been) picked   (nom. pl.)

4. mensā _____ (having been) prepared   (abl. sing.)

5. tēlīs _____ (having been) thrown   (abl. pl.)

6. dōna _____ (having been) promised   (acc. pl.)

7. litterās_____ (having been) written   (acc. pl.)

8. urbis _____ (having been) captured   (gen. sing.)

9. iuvene (masc.)_____ (having been) condemned (dat. sing.)

10. parentibus _____(having been) moved   (dat. pl.)

III. A. **Give a synopsis (see LvO, 154)** 3rd per. sing. of e͞o, -ir͞e, iv͞i or i͞i, ītum:

e.g. Pres. it   he/she/it goes, is going, does go

    Imp. _____   _____

    Fut. _____   _____

    Perf. _____   _____

    PPerf. _____   _____

    FPerf. _____   _____

     B. **Form compounds** of e͞o by prefixing each verb with a **preposition**:

e.g. 1. go to   <u>ade͞o</u>   5. go under   _____

     2. go away   _____   6. go back   _____

     3. go out   _____   7. go across   _____

     4. go in   _____   8. go through _____

                                   (pass away, perish)

IV. A. **Decline** the **interrogative pronoun** <u>quis, quid</u> (see **LvO**, 153):

     <u>SINGULAR</u>   <u>PLURAL</u>

	<u>Masc & Fem</u>	<u>Neut</u>		<u>Masc</u>	<u>Fem</u>	<u>Neut</u>
Nom.	_____	_____		_____	_____	_____
Gen.	_____	_____		_____	_____	_____
Dat.	_____	_____		_____	_____	_____
Acc.	_____	_____		_____	_____	_____
Abl.	_____	_____		_____	_____	_____

V. **Translate** these questions **into English**:

   1. Quis est dea quae est amantibus benigna?

   2. Cuius p͞oma Hippomen͞es in curs͞u i͞ecit?

   3. Cui Hippomen͞es gr͞ati͞as n͞on ͞egit et d͞ona n͞on dedit?

   4. Quem Hippomen͞es am͞ore m͞otus super͞are d͞es͞ider͞avit?

   5. Qu͞o m͞ota, Atalanta Hippomenem mon͞ere tempt͞abat.(Qu͞o=by what)

   6. ͞O, Hippomen͞es, quis t͞e in haec itinera per͞icul͞osa d͞uxit?

   7. ͞A qu͞o Atalanta in m͞atrim͞onium d͞uc͞ebatur?

   8. Qu͞os dea in le͞on͞es transf͞orm͞avit?

VI. **Translate** these verbs in one possible way to show tense **in English**:

1. addūcar
2. prōmittor
3. dūcī (passive infinitive)
4. ītis
5. iēcerit
6. gaudēbant
7. eunt
8. cucurrī
9. īverant
10. adōrāminī

11. īvistī
12. poposcī
13. gaudēte
14. ībam
15. īre
16. adōrābor
17. movērī
18. ībunt
19. ductum
20. poscet

VII. **Translate** these sentences **into English**:

1. Hominēs ab Atalantā victī necābantur.

2. Hostēs hominēs victōs necāvērunt.

3. Senex, ab amīcīs suīs monitus, ad nōs fugiet.

4. Captus nihil dīxit.

5. Nisi meum patrem captum iūverimus, necābitur.

6. Fēminam damnātam nesciō.

7. Librum ā tē missum invenīre nōn potuī.

8. Dē rēbus ab eō factīs audīre dēsīderō.

9. Auxilium prōmissum mātrī dabō.

10. Praemia multa hominibus vulnerātis dare dēbēmus.

Chapter XIX

I. A. **Decline** the **5th declension noun** <u>dies</u> with the **2nd declension**

adjective <u>faustus,</u> a lucky or fortunate day **(see <u>LvO</u>, 162-63)**:

	Singular		Plural	
Nom.	diēs faustus	lucky day	diēs faustī	lucky days
Gen.	_____	_____	_____	_____
Dat.	_____	_____	_____	_____
Acc.	_____	_____	_____	_____
Abl.	_____	_____	_____	_____

Remember, <u>diēs</u> is masculine, except when indicating a particular

day: <u>diē</u> <u>constitūtā</u>, (here <u>diē</u> is abl. fem.), on the day agreed upon.

B. Now **decline** <u>diēs</u> with a **3rd declension adjective** <u>fēlix</u>, a happy

or fortunate day:

Nom.	diēs fēlix	happy day	_____	_____
Gen.	_____	_____	_____	_____
Dat.	_____	_____	_____	_____
Acc.	_____	_____	_____	_____
Abl.	_____	_____	_____	_____

On the New Year one would wish his neighbor "<u>Annum</u> <u>novum</u> <u>faustum</u> <u>et</u> <u>fēlīcem</u>

<u>tibi</u>." The greeting appears on ancient Roman lamps.

II. **Decline a 2nd declension noun** with a **3rd declension adjective:**

(see <u>LvO</u>, 163)

Nom.	omnis vir	every man	omnēs virī	all men
Gen.	_____	_____	_____	_____
Dat.	_____	_____	_____	_____
Acc.	_____	_____	_____	_____
Abl.	_____	_____	_____	_____

III. The **ablative absolute (see <u>LvO</u>, 161-62)** is awkward in its literal translation into English as, "with the battle having been fought," or "with the words having been heard." In better English the ablative absolute would become a **subordinate clause** beginning with a suitable **subordinate conjunction** such as "after, since, because, when, <u>etc</u>." In the sentences below **translate** the ablative absolute first **literally**; then reform it into a more idiomatic English **subordinate clause**:

1. Bellō fīnītō, mīlitēs domum redīvērunt.

   _____, the soldiers returned home.

   _____, the soldiers returned home.

2. Pōmō iactō, Hippomenēs celeriter cucurrit.

   _____, Hippomenes ran swiftly.

   _____, Hippomenes ran swiftly.

3. Vī aureā datā, Midās prīmō gāvīsus est.

   _____, Midas at first rejoiced.

   _____, Midas at first rejoiced.

4. Cibō aureō, Midās nōn iam gāvīsus est.

   _____, Midas no longer rejoiced.

   _____, Midas no longer rejoiced.

5. Saxō iactō, puerī fenestram fractam vīdērunt.

   _____, the boys saw the broken window.

   _____, the boys saw the broken window.

6. Hīs verbīs audītīs, fēminae veniam ōrāvērunt.

   _____, the women begged for pardon.

   _____, the women begged for pardon.

7. Bacchō dūce, hominēs in itinera perīculōsa ductī sunt.

   _____, men were led into dangerous paths.

   _____, men were led into dangerous paths.

(N.B.: The ablative absolute is <u>independent</u> of the main clause.

It is "absolute" because it is not part of the subject or verb.)

Chapter XX

I. A. **Complete** the conjugations below in the **perfect passive (see LvO, 169)**:

līberō (1) free   colō, -ere, coluī, cultum worship

līberātus, -a, -um sum   cultus, -a, -um sum

_____   _____

_____   _____

līberātī, -ae, -a sumus   cultī, -ae, -a sumus

_____   _____

_____   _____

B. **Translate** the **third person singualar** of the forms above:

_____   _____

C. Why is it necessary for the **perfect passive participle** to

be given in **all three genders (see LvO, 170)**?

II. **Translate** each of these **deponent verbs (see LvO, 171)** one way:

1. cōnātur   6. potiēbar
2. locūtus est   7. potiar
3. mirābimur   8. potientur
4. verēbāris   9. mirātus erat
5. loquēminī   10. locūtī sumus

(N.B.: THESE FORMS MUST BE TRANSLATED ACTIVELY!

(see paradigms in LvO, 404-05)

III. **Translate into Latin**:

1. we speak   7. they try
2. we were speaking   8. they were trying
3. we shall   9. they will try
4. we have spoken   10. they have tried
5. we had spoken   11. they had tried
6. we shall have spoken   12. they will have tried

IV. **Fill in** the blanks with the correct form of the intensive **pronoun** or

   adjective īdem, eadem, idem (see <u>LvO</u>, 170-71):

1. <u>The</u> <u>same</u> <u>man</u> appeared at our home. _____

2. We saw <u>the</u> <u>same</u> <u>woman</u> in the theater. _____

3. I like <u>the</u> <u>same</u> <u>things</u> that you do. _____

4. <u>The</u> <u>same</u> <u>men</u> are responsible _____

5. I found it <u>in</u> <u>the</u> <u>same</u> <u>place</u>. _____

6. We called <u>at</u> <u>the</u> <u>same</u> time. _____

7. It is the picture <u>of</u> <u>the</u> <u>same</u> <u>man</u>. _____

8. They gave gifts <u>to</u> <u>the</u> <u>same</u> gods. _____

9. The names <u>of</u> <u>the</u> <u>same</u> gods are familiar. _____

10. We submitted the case <u>to</u> <u>the</u> <u>same</u> judge. _____

V. **Translate** these **5th declension nouns** or **phrases into English**:

   1. rēs pūblica   6. hārum rērum

   2. cum fide (faith)   7. diē constitūtā

   3. in ultimīs diēbus   8. rem pūblicam

   4. diē et nocte   9. spē optimā   (spēs=hope)

   5. fidem maximam   10. rēs gestae

(<u>Res</u> <u>Gestae</u> is the autobiography written by Augustus toward the
end of his life and inscribed on bronze tablets before his tomb.)

VI. **Translate** these sentences **into English**:

   1. Veritī sumus peiōra.

   2. Conāta sum relinquere.

   3. Patior vōbīscum.

   4. Ortus est māne. (<u>māne</u> = early in the morning)

   5. Veritī sunt tyrannum.

   6. Locūtus es cum amīcīs tuīs.

   7. Locūta est cum amīcīs suīs.

   8. Fīlius prō errōribus patris suī passus est.

   9. Fīlius prō errōribus patris suī patī nōn dēbet.

   10. Omnī diē sōl orītur.

Chapter XXI

I. **Give** the **principal parts** and **meaning** of the following verbs:

1. ferō   _____ _____ _____   bear, carry

2. accipiō _____ _____ _____ _____

3. respiciō _____ _____ _____ _____

4. inveniō _____ _____ _____ _____

5. audeō   _____ _____   dare

II. **Give** the English translation for the following **participles (see <u>LvO</u>, 185-86)**;

     identify tense, voice, case, number, and gender (m.,f., or n.):

e.g. 1. ferēns   bearing   pres. act. nom. sing. m.f.n.

2. acceptus _____ _____

3. accipiēns _____ _____

4. recepta _____ _____

5. inventum _____ _____

6. recipiēns _____ _____

7. amātus _____ _____

8. amātūrus _____ _____

9. amantēs _____ _____

10. auferēns _____ _____

11. revertūrus _____ _____

12. audentem _____ _____

III. **Give** the **English translation, case, number** and **use** for each of the
following phrases using **participles** (see <u>LvO</u>, **185-86**):

	Translation	Case, Number, Use
e.g.1. puer crescēns	a growing boy	Nom. Sing. Subj.
2. coniugem plōrantem	_____	_____
3. eī dicentī	_____	_____
4. hīs abientibus	_____	Dat._____
5. cum illīs redientibus	_____	_____
6. eum dicentem	_____	_____
7. eōs dicentēs	_____	_____
8. poētae cantantis	_____	_____
9. deus invocātus	_____	_____
10. carmina cantāta	_____	_____

IV. **Decline** the **3rd declension noun and adjective** <u>ōmen ācre</u> (see <u>LvO</u>, **184-85**):

(Do not confuse the noun <u>ōmen,ōminis</u>, n., omen, with

the adjective <u>omnis, -e</u>, every, all. CAVE!)

Nom.	ōmen ācre	harsh omen	_____ _____
Gen.	ōminis ācris	_____	_____ _____
Dat.	_____	_____	_____ _____
Acc.	_____	_____	_____ _____
Abl.	_____	_____	_____ _____

Our English word "ominous" comes from the genitive of this word.

V. **<u>Ferō</u> and its compounds** are very common Latin verbs.

Review the principal parts of the compounds and **give one possible**

meaning for each of the following forms:

1. abstulit	_____	6. referent	_____
2. relātus	_____	7. lāta	_____
3. attulerat	_____	8. fert	_____
4. ferent	_____	9. tulistis	_____
5. inferunt	_____	10. conferimus	_____

Chapter XXII

I. A. **Give** the **six infinitives** for the verb <u>vocō</u> (1):

	Active		Passive	
Present	vocāre	to call	vocārī	to be called
Perfect	_____	_____	_____	_____
Future	_____	_____	_____	_____

B. **Give** the **six infinitives** for <u>tegō, -ere, texī, tectum</u>:

Present	_____	_____	_____	_____
Perfect	_____	_____	_____	_____
Future	_____	_____	_____	_____

C. **Give** the **six infinitives** for <u>ferō, ferre, tulī, lātum</u>:

Present	_____	_____	_____	_____
Perfect	_____	_____	_____	_____
Future	_____	_____	_____	_____

II. **Translate into English** each of these **infinitives**:

1. ēvēnisse _____
2. fīnīre _____
3. mordērī _____
4. repulsūrus esse _____
5. tectum esse _____
6. doluisse _____
7. lacerātūrum esse _____
8. recognōvisse _____
9. solēre _____
10. lātum esse _____

III. **Fill in** the blanks with forms of the **present infinitive**

to complete the verbs (**complementary infinitive (see <u>LvO</u>, 29)**:

1. a. Quod est perīculōsum, stagnum _____ dēbēmus.

(to cover)

   b. Quod est perīculōsum, stagnum ā nōbīs_____ dēbet.

(to be covered)

2. a. Oppidō vastātō, dominus servōs _____ dēbet.

(to set free = līberāre)

   b. Oppidō vastātō, servī ā dominō _____ dēbent.

(to be set free)

3. a. Servī mensam in domum _____ dēbent.

(to carry: Do not use <u>portāre</u>)

   b. Mensa in domum ā servīs _____dēbet.

(to be carried)

4. a. Hostēs vestrōs _____ dēbētis.

(to love)

   b. Hostēs vestrī ā vōbīs _____ dēbent.

(to be loved)

5. a. Parentēs līberōs suōs _____ dēbent.

(to care for)

   b. Līberī ā parentibus _____ dēbent.

(to be cared for)

IV. **Fill in** the blank with the **future active periphrastic** (note the differ-

ence between the regular future in the first sentence (**see <u>LvO</u>, 193-94**):

1. a. Eurydicē, dente serpentis receptō, occidet.   (will die)

e.g. b. Eurydicē, dente serpentis receptō, <u>occasūra est</u>. (is about to die)

2. a. Orpheus Eurydicen ē Tartarō feret.   (will bring)

   b. Orpheus Eurydicen ē Tartarō _____ .

(is about to bring)

3. a. Orpheus oculōs in Eurydicen reflectet.   (will turn back)

   b. Orpheus oculōs in Eurydicen _____. (is about to turn back)

V. A. What are the **three degrees (see <u>LvO</u>, 195-96)** for each **adjective**?

_____ _____ _____

B. Give three translations for <u>longior, longius</u>:

_____ _____ _____

C. Give three translations for <u>longissumus, -a, -um</u>:

_____ _____ _____

D. **Give** the **comparative and superlative** for the following:

<u>Positive</u>	<u>Comparative</u>	<u>Superlative</u>
1. insānus, -a, -um	_____	_____
2. innocēns, -entis	_____	_____
3. dīversus, -a, -um	_____	_____
4. bonus, -a, -um	_____	_____
5. magnus, -a, -um	_____	_____

VI. **Fill in** the blanks with the **comparative or superlative** forms:

1. ventus _____ (worst)   5. causa _____ (best)

2. iter _____ (better)   6. fidēs _____ (greater)

3. fīlius _____ (smaller)   7. lacrimae _____ (most)

4. praeda _____ (greater)   8. fīlia _____ (smallest)

VII. **Choose** the correct form of the **adverb**:

1. Orpheus sought Eurydice most eagerly.

   Orpheus Eurydicen _____ quaesīvit.

   (avidius / avidissimē)

2. The Bacchantes threw rocks and shouted most loudly.

   Bacchantēs saxa iēcērunt et _____ clamāvērunt.

   (fortius / fortissimē)

3. Orpheus recognized Eurydice in Tartarus most joyfully.

   Orpheus Eurydicen in Tartarō _____ recognōvit.

   (laetius / laetissimē)

MUSICAL CROSSWORD PUZZLE

ACROSS
3. Sounding together pleasantly
6. Increasing in power of tone
8. Quickly
11. Seven performers
12. Very loud
15. Key for score
16. Slowly
20. Very Softly
21. Four performers
22. Regular pulsation
23. Pick
24. Time or beat
25. Performer singing notes above lower range

DOWN
1. Lively
2. Composition with flight of fancy
4. Performer singing deep tones
5. Harmonic resolution
6. With much expression
7. Two performers
9. Loud
10. Soft
13. Six performers
14. Eight performers
17. Three performers
18. Lone performer

Chapter XXIII

I. **Read** the **direct statement**; then **complete** the **indirect statement**

(see **LvO**, 214-16) with an **infinitive**:

1. a. Amīcī nuntiāvērunt, "Iāsōn venit."   (is coming)

e.g. b. Amīcī nuntiāvērunt Iāsonem <u>venīre</u>.   (came)

2. a. Peliās dīxit, "Iter nōn est perīculōsum."   (is not)

  b. Peliās dīxit iter nōn _____ perīculōsum.   (was not)

3. a. Iāsōn putāvit, "Argonautae sunt parātī."   (are ready)

  b. Iāsōn putāvit Argonautās _____ parātōs. (were ready)

II. **Choose** the correct form to complete these **indirect statements**:

1. Iāsōn putāvit iter perīculōsum _____.   (was)

  a. esse   b. fuisse   c. futūrum esse   d. fuit

2. Phrixus putāvit sorōrem _____.   (had died)

  a. mortuus esse b. mortuum esse c. mortuam esse d. erat mortuus

3. Mēdēa dīxit sē Iāsonī auxilium _____. (would give)

  a. dare   b. dedisse   c. datūrum esse   d. datūram esse

III. **Complete** these **indirect statements after a verb of saying**:

1. Dīcunt nāvem _____ tūtam.   (is)
2. Dīcunt nāvem _____ tūtam.   (was)
3. Dīcunt nāvem _____ tūtam.   (will be)
4. Dīxit nāvem _____ tūtam.   (was)
5. Dīxit nāvem _____ tūtam. (had been)
6. Dīxit navem _____ tūtam. (would be)

IV. **Give the Latin** qu<u>ī</u>dam, quaedam, quiddam **(see LvO, 216)** for

"certain" in the following sentences:

1. <u>A</u> <u>certain</u> <u>woman</u> is coming. _____ fēmina
2. I see <u>certain</u> <u>men</u> on the road. _____ homin<u>ē</u>s

(In 1 & 2 forms of qu<u>ī</u>dam, can be used as pronouns.)

3. I gave gifts <u>to certain boys</u>. _____ puer<u>ī</u>s
4. He was saved <u>by a certain slave</u>. <u>ā</u> _____ serv<u>ō</u>
5. These are letters <u>of certain poets</u>. _____ po<u>ē</u>t<u>ā</u>rum
6. A ship was built <u>by a certain Argus</u>. <u>ā</u> _____ Arg<u>ō</u>
7. Pelias feared <u>a certain youth</u>. _____ iuvenem
8. He gave the fleece <u>to a certain king</u>. _____ r<u>ē</u>g<u>ī</u>
9. Jason was told to sow the teeth <u>of a certain dragon</u>.

_____ serpentis

10. <u>Certain queens</u> know how to rule. _____ r<u>ē</u>g<u>ī</u>nae

V. **Decline** s<u>ō</u>lus, -a, -um **(see LvO, 216-17)**:

	Singular			Plural		
Nom	sōlus	sōla	sōlum	____	____	____
Gen	____	____	____	____	____	____
Dat	____	____	____	____	____	____
Acc	____	____	____	____	____	____
Abl	____	____	____	____	____	____

What other adjectives **(see LvO, 422)** are declined like s<u>ō</u>lus?

_____, _____, _____, _____,

_____, _____, _____, _____, _____

An acronym of their first letters spells _____ _____.

Chapter XXIV

I. A. The patterns for forming **present subjunctive (see LvO, 224)** are as follows:

	I	II	III	III-iō	IV
Inf.	amā-re	monē-re	dūce-re	cape-re	sentī-re
	-e-	-ea-	-a-	-ia-	-ia-

    First conjugation gives its **-a-** to **Third**;

      Third conjugation gives its **-e-** to **First**;

        Second conjugation gets both vowels **-ea-**;

          Third -io and fourth conjugation use **-ia-**.

A clever mnemonic* device is the sentence: W**e** h**ea**r **a** l**ia**r.

*Mnemosyne was goddess of memory.   1   2   3,3-iō   4

To these stem endings add the **personal endings** you already know.

  B. **Choose** the correct **present subjunctive** form; write it in the

    blank, and complete a possible translation **(see LvO, 226)**:

1. Vocāmus / Vocēmus   _____ Let us _____

2. Doceat / Docet   _____ Let her _____

3. Dūcās / Dūcis   _____ You may _____

4. Capiō / Capiam   _____ Let me _____

5. Audiant / audiunt   _____ Let them _____

6. Existimētis / Existimātis   _____ You (pl.) may _____

7. Stat / Stet*   _____ Let it _____

8. Sequāminī / Sequiminī   _____ You may _____

9. Arbitrāmur / Arbitrēmur   _____ Let us _____

10. Pōnitur / Pōnātur   _____ Let him _____

11. Committis / Committās   _____ You may _____

12. Concipiam / Concipiō   _____ I may _____

13. Concurrant / Concurrunt   _____ Let them _____

14. Exhortāmur / Exhortēmur   _____ Let us _____

15. Fateor / Fatear   _____ Let me _____

16. Gravāris / Gravēris   _____ You may be _____

17. Nē metuimus / metuāmus   _____ Let us not _____

*Stet is a proofreading code symbol meaning "let it stand" as it was.

II. **Conjugate** the **subjunctive** of <u>sum</u> and <u>possum</u> (see <u>LvO</u>, **224**):

_____ _____ _____ _____

_____ _____ _____ _____

_____ _____ _____ _____

III. **Fill in** the correct **case form** after these **prepositions:**

Piscis in Mari

in + *abl.*
in

trans + *acc.*
across

in + *abl.*
on

sub + *acc.*
under (*or abl.*)

in + *acc.*
into

a (ab) + *abl.*
away from

e (ex) + *abl.*
out of

ad + *acc.*
to, toward,
near

inter + *acc.*
between

ob + *acc.*
against

per + *acc.*
through

circum + *acc.*
around

1. through the water

   per _____

2. into the water

   in _____

3. around the rock

   circum _____

4. in/on the water

   in _____

5. across the water

   trans _____

6. from the rocks

   ā _____

7. to the rocks

   ad _____

8. out of the water

   ex _____

9. between the fish

   inter _____

10. under the rock

    sub_____or____

IV. **Fill in** the blanks with forms of <u>sum</u> or <u>possum</u> (**see <u>LvO</u>, 224**):

    1. Let me be your friend.

    <u>Amīcus tuus</u> _____ .

    2. Let them be able to hear the commands.

    <u>Iussa audīre</u> _____ .

    3. Let me be a witness.

    <u>Testis</u> _____ .

    4. May you be a savior (fem.) for your people!

    <u>Servātrix populō tuō</u> _____ !

    5. May you (pl.) be able to fight back!

    <u>Repugnāre</u> _____ .

    6. Let him not be ungrateful!

    <u>Nē ingrātus</u> _____ !

    7. Let us be safe.

    <u>Salvī</u> _____ .

    8. Let them be able to sail tomorrow.

    <u>Crās nāvigāre</u> _____ .

V. **Fill in** the blanks with the letter of the **word(s) with the opposite meaning**:

_____ 1. dēterior	a. in perīculō
_____ 2. nefārius	b. multī
_____ 3. brevis	c. miser
_____ 4. paucī	d. falsus
_____ 5. minor	e. benignus
_____ 6. vērus	f. maior
_____ 7. ingrātus	g. honestus
_____ 8. saevus	h. grātus
_____ 9. salvus	i. longus
_____ 10. fēlix	j. melior

VI. A. Medea's Dilemma: Medea wrestles with herself over her love for Jason and her loyalty to her father. **Fill in** the appropriate **subjunctive** (S) or **future ending** (F) of the verb:

Contrā Iāsonem

e.g. 1. Occidat!   (S) 1. Let him die!

    2. Nē patrem trād_____   (S) 2. Let me not betray my father.

    3. Vir alterius s_____.   (S) 3. He may be the husband of another.

    4. Fidem d_____.   (S) 4. Let him give his promise.

    5. Relinqu_____-ne patriam? (F) 5. Shall I leave my country?

Pro Iāsone

    1. Vīvat!   (S) 1. Let him live!

    2. Hunc advenam am____.   (S) 2. Let me love this stranger.

    3. Meus vir s_____.   (S) 3. Let him be my husband.

    4. Dī testēs s_____.   (S) 4. May the gods be witnesses.

    5. Terram meliorem nosc____.(F) 5. I shall get to know a better land.

B. What is the spelling of the **first person singular, future indicative** in the third, third-iō, and fourth conjugation?

        trād_____,   cap_____,   ven_____

Note that the **first person singular, present subjunctive for these same verbs is spelled the same:**

        trād_____,   cap_____,   ven_____

VII. **Indicate** the **opposite idea** of the words in the first column:

_____ 1. mens or anima   a. frāter

_____ 2. timor   b. nox

_____ 3. germāna   c. amor <u>or</u> commōtiō (<u>emotion</u>)

_____ 4. ratiō   d. caelum

_____ 5. furor   e. virtus <u>or</u> fortitūdō

_____ 6. tellūs   f. mens sāna

_____ 7. nāta   g. arātrum (<u>plowshare</u>)

_____ 8. ferrum   h. initium (<u>beginning</u>)

_____ 9. exitum   i. corpus

_____ 10. diēs   j. fīlius <u>or</u> nātus

Chapter XXV

I. What is the formula for the **imperfect subjunctive (see LvO, 234)**?

_____ + _____ , both active and passive

e.g. I amāret; II habēret; III dūceret; III-iō faceret; IV venīret

   amārētur; habērētur; dūcērētūr; facerētur;   venīrētur

II. **Fill in** the **imperfect subjunctive** for these verbs (**Lvo, 234**):

1. nāvigō   3rd per. sing. act.   nāvigāret

2. maneō   3rd per. pl. act.   _____

3. mittō   1st per. sing. act.   _____

4. faciō   3rd per. sing. pass.   _____

5. sentiō   2nd per. pl. act.   _____

6. cadō   2nd per. sing. act.   _____

7. ardō   3rd per. pl. pass.   _____

8. discō   3rd per. sing. act.   _____

9. convertō 1st per. pl. pass.   _____

10. effugiō   1st per. sing. act.   _____

III. **Fill in** the blanks with the correct form of the **imperfect subjunctive** in these **purpose clause (see LvO, 234-35)** sentences. Note that the literal "so that she might receive" is often translated as "to receive":

e.g. 1. Mēdēa in silvās īvit ut herbās magicās <u>reciperet</u>.

   Medea went into the woods to receive magic potions (herbs).

2. Iāsōn prōmīsit ut Mēdēam in mātrimōnium _____. (to lead)

3. Iāsōn mātrimōnium prōmīsit ut Mēdēa eī auxilium _____.

   (might give)

4. Iāsōn iugum in taurōs posuit ut agrum _____. (to plow)

5. Iāsōn saxum inter virōs iēcit ut bellum ā sē _____ . (to turn)

6. Mēdēa carmina dedit ut grātiās deīs _____.

   (to thank = <u>grātiās</u> <u>agere</u>)

7. Iāsōn vēnerat ut vellere aureō _____.

   (to get possession of = <u>potīrī</u>, deponent verb)

IV. **Fill in** the correct form of the **imperfect subjunctive** in these

sentences containing **result clauses** (<u>LvO</u>, 235), and **translate**:

1. Fēmina tot līberōs habēbat ut satis cibī nōn _____.

                                                    (she did ... have)

2. Mēdēa tantum amōrem habēbat ut Iāsonī auxilium _____.

                                                 (she gave)

3. Aeētēs tot labōrēs Iāsonī dedit ut hērōs maximē _____.

                                                 (feared)

4. Iāsōn erat tam fōrmōsus ut Mēdēa statim eum _____.

                                                 (loved)

5. Draco erat tam horrendus ut nēmō vellere aureō potīrī _____.

                                                 (could)

V. The **imperfect subjunctive** for **deponent verbs** is unusual in

that the **missing active infinitive form** has to be restored

in order for the **passive personal endings** to be added:

    e.g. <u>hortārētur</u>, so that he might urge

<u>hort-</u>	<u>-āre-</u>	<u>-tur</u>	>	<u>hortārētur</u>
stem	missing	passive personal		-ē long before <u>-tur</u>
	infinitive	ending		

Fill in the blanks with the **English translation** for the Latin

imperfect subjunctive in 1-5; **translate 6-10 into Latin**:

e.g. 1. ut sequerētur   so that he/she/it might follow

    2. ut cōnārēmur   _____

    3. ut hortārēminī   _____

    4. ut potīrentur   _____

    5. ut nāscerer   _____

    6. so that he might confess   (ut fateor)_____

    7. so that they might judge   (ut arbritror)_____

    8. so that you (s.) might be born (ut nascor)_____

    9. so that you (pl.) might die   (ut morior)_____

    10. so that I might set out   (ut egredior)_____

Etymology Games

I. **Match** up these legal terms (see <u>LvO</u>, 238-39):

1. habeās corpus   ___ a. friend of the court

2. causā mortis   ___ b. the situation speaks for itself

3. amīcus cūriae   ___ c. the body in the crime

4. inter vīvōs   ___ d. (a gift given) when the

5. prīmā faciē   donor is near death

6. rēs ipsa loquitur   ___ e. voluntarily

7. suā sponte   ___ f. in or of the thing itself

8. nōlō contendere   ___ g. on the face of it

9. in rem   (at first appearance)

10. corpus delictī   ___ h. during the lifetime

                           ___ i. a writ to obtain a person's body

                           ___ j. I do not wish to contend the charge

II. **Match** these anatomical or medical terms (see <u>LvO</u>, 248-49):

1. capillary   ___ a. a bending muscle

2. nasal   ___ b. unborn offspring

3. oral   ___ c. dog or tooth

4. ocular   ___ d. pertaining to throat/neck

5. lacrimal   ___ e. pertaining to the stomach

6. aural   ___ f. pertaining to the nose

7. jugular   ___ g. pertaining to the arm

8. bracchial   ___ h. pertaining to the eye

9. flexor   ___ i. pertaining to the mouth

10. pectoral   ___ j. pertaining to the chest

11. foetus, fetus   ___ k. pertaining to the ear

12. ventral   ___ l. pertaining to tears

13. canine   ___ m. resembling a hair

Chapter XXVI

I. **Write** the formula for the **perfect subjunctive**:

Active: _____ stem + _____ of <u>sum</u>, except for <u>-erō</u> > <u>-erim</u>

                          (written as one word)

Conj.	I	II	III	III-iō	IV
e.g.	vocāverim	docuerim	mīserim	fēcerim	sēnserim

Passive: _____ _____ _____ + _____ _____ of sum

                          (written as two words)

e.g. vocātus sit   doctus sit   missus sit   factus sit   sēnsus sit

II. **Give** the **Tense, Person, Number, and Voice** for these **Perfect Subjuctive verbs** and note one possible translation:

	Tense	Per.	Num.	Voice	Translation
1. ut ascenderit					that she ascended
2. ut secueritis					that you (pl) cut
3. ut vocāverimus					that we called
4. ut vulnerāta sit					that she was wounded

III. Write the formula for the **pluperfect subjunctive (see <u>LvO</u>, 245)**:

Active: _____ inf_____ + _____ _____

                (written as one word)

e.g. vocāvissem   docuissem   mīsissem   fēcissem   sēnsissem

Passive: _____ _____ _____ + _____ _____ of sum

                (written as two words)

e.g. vocātus esset _____ _____ _____ _____

IV. **List Tense, Person, and Number** for these verbs: note translation:

	Tense	Per.	Num.	Voice	Translation
1. sī dormīvissem					if I had slept
2. sī micāvissent					if they had shone
3. sī expertus esset					if he had tried
4. sī recēpissem					if I had received

64

V. **Match** the **associated ideas** in Column I with those in Column II:

e.g. 1. āla   _1_ a. volucris or avis   (bird)

2. aēnus   ___ b. arbor   (tree)

3. barba   ___ c. sacerdōs   (priest)

4. certāmen cursūs   ___ d. gladiātor   (gladiator)

5. ensis   ___ e. Circus Maximus

6. lac   ___ f. mānēs   (shades of the dead)

7. olīva   ___ g. agnus   (lamb)

8. ovis   ___ h. pōmum pressum   (squeezed)

9. sepulchrum   ___ i. gallīna   (chicken)

10. prex   ___ j. vacca   (cow)

11. ōvum   ___ k. senex   (old man)

12. sūcus   ___ l. coquus   (cook)

VI. **Supply** the correct form of the **imperfect** or **pluperfect subjunctive** in these **contrary-to-fact sentences (see LvO, 245-46)**:

1. If Jason loved with Medea, he would marry her.

Sī Iāsōn Mēdēam _____, eam in mātrimōnium _____.

2. If Jason had truly loved Medea, he would not have left her.

Sī Iason Mēdēam vērē _____, eam nōn _____.

3. If Medea were not able to do it, she would not change Aeson into a young man.

Nisi Mēdēa hoc facere _____, Aesonem in iuvenem nōn _____.

4. If Medea had not been able to do it, she would not have changed Aeson into a young man.

Nisi Mēdēa hoc facere _____, Aesonem in iuvenem nōn _____.

5. If Aeetes had followed the lovers, he would have killed Jason.

Sī Aeētēs amantēs _____ _____, Iāsonem _____.

VII. A. What is the most common use of the **dative case** that you have

so far encountered? _____ _____

B. The dative case is also used with **certain verbs** which imply a

"to" or "for" idea in their meaning **(see LvO, 246, 412-13)**.

Some verbs governing the dative are **compound verbs**. What is a

compound verb?_____

C. **Choose** the proper **Latin** object in the following sentences that

demonstrate most of the uses of the **dative case**:

1. Give thanks to me, not to Minerva.

   (Mihi/Mē), nōn (Minervae/Minervam) grātiās da! _____ _____

2. I owe my safety to you.

   (Tibi/ Ad tē) salūtem meam dēbeō. _____

3. Believe me!

   Credite (mē/ mihi)! _____

4. Forgive them, father!

   Ignosce, pater, (illōs/ illīs)! _____

5. He commands the soldiers.

   (Mīlitēs/ Mīlitibus) imperat. _____

6. Medea wanted to harm Theseus.

   (Thēseum/ Thēseō) Mēdēa nocēre voluit _____

7. The king wants to spare his son.

   (Fīlium/ Fīliō) rēx parcēre vult. _____

8. The leader was in charge of the army.

   Dux (exercituum/ exercituī) praefuit. _____

9. Come tomorrow, if you please.

   Venīte crās, sī (vōs/ vōbīs) placet. _____

Chapter XXVII

I. A. How many tenses are in **indicative mood**? ___ In **subjunctive**?___

List the tenses in the **indicative**:   In the **subjunctive**:

_____   _____

_____   _____

_____

_____   _____

_____   _____

_____

Why are there **no future tenses** in the **subjunctive mood**?

_____

B. **Give a synopsis** of <u>mittō</u> in the **subjunctive**, 3rd sing.,

active and passive:

	<u>Active</u>	<u>Passive</u>
Pres.	mittat	_____
Imp.	_____	_____
Perf.	_____	_____
PPerf.	_____	_____

<u>**REMEMBER THAT MANY TRANSLATIONS OF THE SUBJUNCTIVE ARE POSSIBLE.**</u>

II. Fill in the Latin **interrogative word(s)** for each of these **direct questions**:

1. Who are you?   1. _____ es?

2. What is she doing?   2. _____ facit?

3. Why is she coming?   3. _____ venit?

4. Where are they training? 4. _____ exercent?

5. Where is the Isthmus?   5. _____ _____ est Isthmus?

6. When is the race?   6. _____ est certāmen?

7. How does Theseus win?   7. _____ Thēsēus vincit?

III. **Change** each **direct question** in Exercise II above into an **indirect question (see LvO, 261)** by introducing it with <u>Scit</u> (He knows) in the main clause and by **changing the verb in the subordinate clause** to **subjunctive**:

1. Scit quis <u>sīs</u>.　　　　　　1. He knows who you are.

2. Scit quid <u>faciat</u>.　　　　　2. He knows what she is doing.

3. Scit cūr _____.　　　　3. He knows _____.

4. Scit ubi _____.　　　　4. He knows _____.

5. Scit quō locō Isthmus _____.　5. He knows _____.

6. Scit quandō certāmen _____.　6. He knows _____.

7. Scit quōmodō Thēseus _____. 7. He knows _____.

IV. All of the indirect questions above are in **primary sequence** because <u>Scit</u> is in the **present tense**. **Change** <u>Scit</u> to <u>Scīvit</u> and the verbs in the subordinate clause to the **imperfect subjunctive**; you are now in **secondary sequence (see LvO, 261-62)**:

1. Scīvit quis essēs.　　　　　1. He knew who you were.

2. Scīvit _____ _____.　2. _____.

3. Scīvit _____ _____.　3. _____.

4. Scīvit _____ _____.　4. _____.

5. Scīvit _____ Isthmus _____. 5. _____.

6. Scīvit _____ certāmen _____. 6. _____.

7. Scīvit _____ Thēseus _____. 7. _____.

V. Now **Change** each sentence above to **secondary sequence** using the **pluperfect tense** of the verb in the **subordinate clause.**

1. Scīvit quis fuissēs.　　　　1. He knew who you had been.

2. _____.　　　　2. _____.

3. _____.　　　　3. _____.

4. _____.　　　　4. _____.

5. _____ Isthmus _____.　5. _____.

6. _____ certāmen _____.　6. _____.

7. _____ Thēseus _____.　7. _____.

VI. From what Latin verb does the name for the **locative case** come?

_____ meaning _____

Complete each sentence with the proper form of the **locative** or

the **accusative** with or without a preposition **(see LvO, 262-63)**:

1. _____ ībam.   (to Rome)   5. _____ nāvigāmus.   (to Africa)

2. _____ habitat. (in Rome)   6. _____ habitāmus.   (in Africa)

3. _____ labōrās.(in Athens)   7. _____ habitāmus.   (at home)

4. _____ habitō. (on Sicily)   8. _____ habitō.   (in the country)

(a large island)

CROSSWORD PUZZLE WITH RELIGIOUS TERMS **(see LvO, 264-65)**

ACROSS
  1. Coming
  4. Ceremony: being strengthened
  5. Habitation for nuns
  6. Sharing ceremony: blood and body
  9. Raised place for worship
12. Turning to a new religion
14. Sayings: "Blessed are ...."
15. Evening prayers
16. Garment worn by a priestly person
17. Written testimony
18. Biblical order

DOWN
  1. Going up to heaven
  2. Blessing
  3. Beginning
  5. flock
  7. Admission of sin
  8. Heavenly messenger
10. Flock
11. I believe; my belief
13. Being made

Chapter XXVIII

I.A. **Name two parts of speech** as possiblities for the word **cum (LvO, 271)**:

a prep_____ meaning _____, or a subordinate _____ meaning

_____, _____, _____, or _____.

B. In the following sentences **tell** whether cum is a **preposition (P)**

or a **subordinate conjunction (SC)**, and **write** its Enlish meaning in

the blank at the end of the line:

P or SC   Translation

_____ 1. In urbe cum paucīs amīcīs revēnit.   _____

_____ 2. Litterās tuās magnō cum gaudeō respondeō.   _____

_____ 3. Cum Mēdēa Thēseum vīdit, eum recognōvit.   _____

_____ 4. Magnō cum amōre Mēdēa Thēseum iūvit.   _____

_____ 5. Thēseus dubitat cum saxum videt.   _____

_____ 6. Cum Thēseus in rēgiam inīret, Mēdēa eum   _____

occīdere cōnāta est.

_____ 7. Mēdēa magnopere timēbat cum facinus pateret.   _____

_____ 8. Aegeus mirātus est cum Thēseum esse fīlium   _____

invenīret.

_____ 9. Cum amīcīs ad īnsulam novum Thēseus nāvigāvit.   _____

_____10. Mīnōs bellum preparāvit cum fīlius Androgeus   _____

interfectus esset.

II. In clauses where cum governs the **subjunctive (see LvO, 271)**, there are

several possible translations: when, since, because, or although. **Decide**

which is the best meaning for cum, and **translate** each sentence **into English**:

1. Cum Thēseus pōculum ā rēge sūmeret, Aegeus ornāmentum gladiī

recognōvit.

_____

2. Cum fīlius inventus esset, rēx magnopere gāvīsus est.

_____

3. Cum Mēdēa facinus patēre vidēret, magnopere timēbat et relinquere voluit.

_____

4. Cum isthmus pacātus esset, tamen cīvēs taurum album timēbant.

_____

5. Cum Androgeus necātus esset, Mīnōs imperāvit ut septem
    iuvenēs et septem virginēs Crētam mitterentur.

_____

_____

6. Cum biforme monstrum Pāsiphaē nātum esset, Mīnōs proelem sub
    rēgia cēlāre cōnātus est.

_____

7. Cum septem iuvenēs et virginēs sorte (by lot) lectī essent,
    tamen Thēsēus quoque cum illīs īre constituit.

_____

8. Quae cum ita sint, Aegeus miserrimus fīlium ēgredī videt.
   Since these things are so,_____

9. Cum pax in urbe esset, hominēs facilius labōrāre poterant.

_____

III. **Fill in** the **dative case** (see <u>LvO</u>, 73, 271) **with adjectives**:

      1. Thēsēus erat _____ cārus   (to his father)

      2. Rēs nōn erat _____ grāta.   (to Medea)

      3. Thēsēus erat fīlius _____ ignārus. (to his parent)

71

IV. **Fill in** the **comparative** and **superlative** of these **adjectives**:

(see <u>LvO</u>, 195-96, 271-72, 422)

Positive	Comparative	Superlative
1. longus, -a, -um	_____	_____
2. facilis, -e	_____	_____
3. difficilis -e	_____	_____ _____
4. miser, -era, -erum	_____	_____
5. sacer, -cra, -crum	_____	_____
6. ācer, ācris, ācre	_____	_____
7. bonus, -a, -um	_____	_____
8. malus, -a, -um	_____	_____
9. parvus, -a, -um	_____	_____
10. magnus, -a, -um	_____	_____
11. multus, -a, -um	_____	_____

V. **Fill in** the blanks with the proper **comparative** or **superlative**:

1. May the best man win!
1. _____ vincat!

2. The easiest path is often the worst.
2. Iter _____ saepe est _____.

3. The hardest path is often the best.
3. Iter _____ saepe est _____.

4. The best things in life are without price.
4. In vītā _____ sunt sine pretiō.

5. The most sacred temple has been burned.
5. Templum _____ arsum est.

6. Worse men cannot be found.
6. _____ (hominēs) invenīrī nōn possunt.

7. The sun is brighter than the moon.
7. Sōl est _____ quam lūna. (<u>or</u> lūna <u>without</u> quam)

Chapter XXIX

I. **Decline** the **relative pronoun quī, quae, quod (see LvO, 143)**:

	Singular			English	Plural		
Nom.	quī	quae	quod	who, what	quī	quae	quae
Gen.	_____	_____	_____	_____	_____	_____	_____
Dat.	_____	_____	_____	_____	_____	_____	_____
Acc.	_____	_____	_____	_____	_____	_____	_____
Abl.	_____	_____	_____	_____	_____	_____	_____

II. A **relative pronoun** introduces an adjectival descriptive clause modifying a noun. The relative pronoun refers to this noun in the main clause. The noun is called the _____. The relative pronoun **must agree with this noun** in _____ and _____, but **it takes its case from its use in its own clause.**

Underline the **antecedent** in each sentence below; then **choose** the correct pronoun from the choices given:

1. Pāsiphaē, _____ erat coniūnx Mīnōis, taurum amāvit.

   a. cui   b. quae   c. quod   d. cuius

2. Biforme monstrum, _____ Pāsiphaē tulit, erat pudor Mīnōi.

   a. qui   b. quae   c. quod   d. cui

3. Mīnōs, _____ hunc pudōrem removēre voluit, Mīnōtaurum sub rēgiā cēlāvit.

   a. quī   b. quae   c. quod   d. quem

4. Daedalus, _____ Mīnōs opus labyrinthum aedificandī dedit, erat celeberrimus in hāc arte.

   a. quem   b. quod   c. quam   d. cui

5. Daedalus labyrinthum aedificāvit, in _____ Mīnōs Mīnōtaurum cēlāre constituit.

   a. quī   b. quō   c. quā   d. cui

6. Iuvenēs, _____ sorte lectī sunt, Crētam mittēbantur.

   a. quibus   b. quōrum   c. quī   d. quae

73

7. Nāvis albō vēlō nāvigābit, _____ erit signum Aegeō.

    a. quod   b. quae   c. quārum   d. quae

8. Thēseus ānulum rettulit _____ Mīnōs in mare iēcerat.

    a. quod   b. quae   c. quem   d. cui

9. Ariadna, _____ auxiliō Thēseus effūgit, erat fīlia rēgis.

    a. quae   b. quod   c. quem   d. cuius

10. Iuvenēs, _____ Thēseus servāverat, cum hērōe effūgērunt.

    a. quās   b. quōs   c. quibus   d. quōrum

11. Ariadna, _____ Thēseūs in Diā relīquerat, ā Bacchō servāta est.

    a. quem   b. quae   c. quam   d. cui

III. In each of the sentences above, **tell** the **gender** and **number** of the **antecedent**, and the **case** and **use** of the **relative pronoun**:

	Antecedent	Gender	Number	Relative Pronoun	Case & Use
e.g. 1.	Pāsifaē	Fem.	Sing.	quae	Nom. Subj.
2.	_____			_____	
3.	_____			_____	
4.	_____			_____	
5.	_____			_____	
6.	_____			_____	
7.	_____			_____	
8.	_____			_____	
9.	_____			_____	
10.	_____			_____	

IV. **Translate** these sentences **into English. Note the difference** when the **verb** in the **relative clause of characteristic** is **subjunctive** (see <u>LvO</u>, 280-81):

1. Mīnōs erat rēx quī Mīnōtaurum cēlāret.

    _____

2. Thēseus erat hērōs quī Mīnōtaurum occīderet.

    _____

3. Aegeus erat parēns quī fīliō necātō sē occīderet.

    _____

4. Thēseus fēminam amāvit quae auxilium daret.

_____

5. Thēseus iuvenibus fīlum mōnstrāvit quō effugerent.

_____

V. The **impersonal verbs** are sometimes best translated by an

English idiom **(see LvO, 281, 336)**. First **give the literal translation,**

then the **more idiomatic English**:

1. Licet vōbīs fūmāre in hōc locō.   (fūmāre = to smoke)

_____

_____

2. Libet discipulīs librōs legere.

_____

_____

3. Oportet discipulōs studēre, sī discere dēsīderant.

_____

_____

4. Placet mihi hās litterās tibi scrībere.

_____

_____

5. Oportet amīcōs habēre, sī laetī esse vultis.

_____

_____

6. Licet vōbīs lūdere postquam labōrātis.

_____

_____

7. Nullī umquam licet scīre quid ageret.

_____

_____

VI. A. What **part of speech** is a gerund (<u>LvO</u>, 282-83)? _____ _____

    B. In what cases is the **gerund** declined? _____, _____, _____, ____

    C. What takes the place of the **gerund** in the nominative: _____

    D. What three letters indicate the **genitive gerund**? _____

    E. How is the **gerund <u>aedificandī</u>** translated? _____

    F. **Translate** these phrases **into English**:

       1. amor discendi   _____

       2. spēs effugiendī   _____

       3. facultās sanandī (heal   _____

       4. ars decipiendī   _____

       5. amor currendī   _____

       6. amor aedificandī   _____

       7. ars construendī   _____

       8. ars docendī   _____

       9. opportūnitās vincendī   _____

      10. tempus nascendī   _____

      11. tempus moriendī   _____

G. **Persons** with the skills or interests listed above appear below. **Change** the first word in each phrase above into the **accusative case**, **object** of the verb of having:

e.g. 1. Discipulus <u>amōrem discendī</u> habet.

    2. Servī _____ habent.

    3. Medicī _____ habent.   <u>medicus</u>=doctor

    4. Magī _____ habent.   <u>magus</u>=magician

    5. Cursōrēs _____ habent.   <u>cursor</u>=racer

    6. Architectī _____ habent.   <u>architectus</u>=architect

    7. Structōrēs _____ habent. <u>structor</u>=builder,mason

    8. Magister _____ habet.

    9. Imperātor _____ habet.

   10. Omnēs _____ habent.

   11. Hērōs _____ habet.

Chapter XXX

I. A. **Give** the **principal parts** of <u>volō</u>, _____, _____, want **(see <u>LvO</u>, 289-90).**

   B. **Conjugate** <u>volō</u> in   C. **Give a synopsis** of <u>volō</u>, 3rd sing.

   the **present tense**:   <u>Indicative</u>   <u>Subjunctive</u>

1   volō   Pres.   _____   _____

2   _____   Imp.   _____   _____

3   _____   Fut.   _____

1   _____   Perf.   _____   _____

2   _____   PPerf.   _____   _____

3   _____   Futperf. _____

   D. 1. How do you say, "you do not want?" both sing. _____

                and pl. _____

      2. How do you say, "he does not want?" _____

      3. How do you say, "we prefer?" _____

II. A. **Give** the **imperative** singular and plural of <u>nōlō</u>: _____ _____

   B. How are these words used in Latin? _____

   C. **Translate into Latin:**

     1. Do not force. (sing.)   _____

     2. Do not disturb! (pl.)   _____

     3. Do not beg. (sing.)   _____

     4. Do not forget me. (pl.)   _____ (forget + gen.)

     5. Do not answer. (sing.)   _____

   D. **Translate into English:**

     1. Cīvēs commovēre nōluī. _____

     2. Māluimus oblīviscī proeliī. _____

     3. Nōlēbat habērī* imperātor. _____

     4. Bona nōn mala mālint! _____

     5. Sī uxor dōna pretiōsissima nōluisset, vir eam nōn relīquisset.

   _____

   *The passive of <u>habere</u> often means "to be considered."

III. **Supply** the verb in **imperfect or pluperfect subjunctive** in

these **noun clauses of desire** (**LvO**, 290-91) (in **secondary sequence**):

1. Multī Thēseum ōrāvērunt ut auxilium _____.

(to give)

2. Rēx populō imperāvit ut templa sacra _____.

(to decorate)

3. Calydōn hērōes implōrāvit ut ingentem suem _____.

(to kill)

4. Antigonē rēgem ōrāvit ut corpus frātris _____.

(to bury)

5. Principēs Thēseum rogābat ut in bellō contrā Thēbānōs

_____.

(to help)

IV. **Select** the correct **subjunctive verb** in these **clauses within indirect**

statement (see **LvO**, 291-92):

1. He said that the slaves who helped ought to be freed.

Dīxit servōs quī (adiūvērunt/adiūvārent) līberārī dēbent.

2. We knew that you who preferred exile did not wish death.

Scīvimus tē quī exilium (mālēbās/māllēs) mortem nōlle.

3. They thought that he who was a prince was a strong leader.

Putābant illum quī princeps (erat/esset) dūx fortis esse.

4. You said that the Amazon whom Theseus loved was Hippolyta.

Dīxistī Amazōnem quem Thēseūs (amābat/amāret) esse

Hippolytam.

5. Theseus hoped that Hercules whom he always admired would

return to sanity.

Thēseūs sperābat Herculem quem semper (mīrābātur/mīrārētur)

in mentem sanam reventūrum esse.

LEGAL LATIN CROSSWORD PUZZLE (see **LvO**, 238-39)

ACROSS

3. In or of the thing itself
4. On one side only
6. I do not wish to contend
12. By family branches
13. Friend of the court
14. Of one's own will

DOWN

1. Equal participation
2. Writ to obtrain a person's body
3. During the lifetime
5. The situation speaks for itself
7. Cause of death
8. On the face of it (at first glance)
9. Now for then
10. Beyond the powers defined
11. Under penalty to produce

Chapter XXXI

LATIN POETRY (see <u>LvO</u>, 310-11 and Appendix B, 447-52)

I. A. What is the **meter** of Roman **epic** literature? _____

  B. Give the scheme for each foot: **dactyl**_____; **spondee**_____

  C. What is meant by **hexameter**? _____

  D. A **syllable is** considered **long** if it contains 1.a_____vowel

                                       2.<u>a</u>_____

                 3.<u>a</u>_____vowel <u>followed by</u>_____

  E. What is **elision**? _____. Where does it occur?

  _____

  F. What is meant by **caesura**?_____

  G. **Scan** the lines referring to Ulysses' power to sway Agamemnon:

  (Scan = mark the long and short syllables and the six feet)

    atque in rēge tamen pater est; ego mīte parentis

    ingenium verbīs ad publica commoda vertī:

    difficilem tenuī sub inīquō iūdice causam.

    Hunc tamen utilitās populī frāterque datīque

    summa movet sceptrī, laudem ut cum sanguine penset;

II. **Give** the full forms and meaning for these **poetic contractions** (see <u>LvO</u>, 311):

	<u>Full</u> Form	<u>Meaning</u>
1. vīdēre <	_____	_____
2. parāssent <	_____	_____
3. mutāsse <	_____	_____
4. fore	_____	_____

III. **Give** the **present tense** of <u>fīō, fierī</u>, become, and <u>eō, īre</u>, go:

  <u>fīō</u> _____ _____ _____ _____ _____

  <u>eō</u> _____ _____ _____ _____ _____

IV. **Give a synopsis** of fĭō and eō both **indicative** and **subjunctive, 3rd person**

   Singular (see LvO, 335, 433-36):

	Indicative	Subjunctive	Indicative	Subjunctive
Pres.	_fit_	_____	_it_	_____
Imp.	_____	_____	_____	_____
Fut.	_____		_____	
Perf.	_____	_____	_____	_____
Pperf.	_____	_____	_____	_____
FPerf.	_____		_____	

V. **Translate into English** these sentences that use forms of fĭō:

   1. Paris hērōs magnus numquam factus est.

   2. Neptūnus violentus in undīs fiēbat.

   3. Agamemnon dux Graecōrum factus est.

   4. Aegeō mortuō, Thēseus rēx Athēnīs factus est.

   5. Iphigenīa sacrificium virginī deae facta est.

   6. Fīat lūx; et erat lūx.

VI. **Translate** these sentences **into English**, giving force to the **real conditions**

   (see LvO, 309):

1. Sī Paris pōmum aureum Venerī dederit, dea eī pulcherrimam fēminam dabit.

   _____

2. Sī Paris Spartam ībit, ipse Helenam vidēbit.

   _____

3. Sī Paris Helenam vīderit, eam dēsīderābit.

   _____

4. Sī Paris Helenam dēsīderābit, eam rapiet.

   _____

5. Si Paris Helenam rapuerit, bellum inter Graecōs et Trōiānōs fiet.

   _____

The verbs in both clauses of these **real conditions** use the **future** or **future perfect**

indicative. This use is sometimes called the **Future More Vivid.**

VII. **Change** each of these **contrary-to-fact conditions** from the
imperfect to the **pluperfect subjunctive** and notice the change
in the English meaning **(see LvO, 310)**:

e.g. 1. Sī Paris nōn Helenam <u>raperet</u>, bellum nōn <u>esset</u>.

If Paris <u>were</u> not <u>carrying off</u> Helen, there <u>would</u> not <u>be</u> war.

Sī Paris nōn Helenam <u>rapuisset</u>, bellum nōn <u>fuisset</u>.

If Paris <u>had</u> not <u>carried off</u> Helen, there <u>would</u> not <u>have been</u> war.

2. Nisi ventī saevī Aulide aequora invia <u>facerent</u>, Danaī Trōiam <u>navigarent</u>.

_____

Nisi venti saevi Aulide aequora invia _____, Danai Troiam _____.

_____

3. Si Aiax ad Clytemnestram <u>iret</u>, mater Iphigeniam non <u>mitteret</u>.

_____

Si Aiax ad Clytemnestram _____, māter Iphigenīam nōn _____.

_____

4. Nisi Agamemnōn fīliam <u>sacrificāret</u>, Dīāna ventōs nōn <u>mūtāret</u>.

_____

Nisi Agamemnōn fīliam _____, Dīāna ventōs nōn _____

_____

5. Nisi linguae Latīnae <u>studērētis</u>, hanc fābulam nōn <u>legerētis</u>.

_____

Nisi linguae Latīnae _____, hanc fābulam nōn _____.

_____

VIII. **Insert** the **present subjunctive** forms in these **should-would clauses** (also
known as the **Future Less Vivid, see LvO, 310**):

Sī Paris _____, Menelāus eum _____.
      (should return)   (would kill)

Sī Helena _____, Menelāus eī _____.
      (should return)   (would forgive=<u>ignoscere</u> ± <u>dat.</u>)

IX. **Roman months** were named after gods, events, rulers, or numbers.

A. The original year of 10 months began with March. **Study** the list of

    etymologies in <u>LvO</u>, 313, and **give** an **etymology** for each month:

    1. March   _____

    2. April   _____ or _____

    3. May   _____ or _____

    4. June   _____ or _____

    5. July   _____, originally _____, the ____th

    6. August   _____, originally _____, the ____th

    7. September   _____

    8. October   _____

    9. November   _____

    10. December   _____

B. The addition of **two months before March** accounts for our present

    calendar being two months different in the last four months from

    their numerical source. Give an **etymology** for these two months:

    1. January   _____ Why is this an appropriate god?

    2. February   _____, days of _____

C. Romans indicated the date as being on or so many days before

    three points in the month: **Kalends, Nones, and Ides. Give** the

    day for each of these points in the month **(see <u>LvO</u>, 440):**

    1. Kalends   _____ source of English word _____

    2. Nones   ____ or ____

    3. Ides   ____ or ____

Write the poem that tells which months have certain days for

Nones and Ides (see <u>LvO</u>, 440):

    <u>In March, July, October, May,</u>   _____

    _____   _____

D. **Convert** the following **Roman dates** to **present dates:**

    Kal. Iān. _____ Nōn. Māi._____ Īd. Mar. _____

    What event took place Īd. Mar.? _____

Chapter XXXII

I. **Give** a **synopsis** of these **deponent verbs** as indicated (**LvO,** 318-19):

	3rd Sing. cōnor, -ārī, -ātus sum		3rd Pl. sequor, -ī, secūtus sum	
	Indicative	Subjunctive	Indicative	Subjunctive
Pres.	_____	_____	_____	_____
Imp.	_____	_____	_____	_____
Fut.	_____		_____	
Perf.	_____	_____	_____	_____
Pperf.	_____	_____	_____	_____
Fperf.	_____		_____	

II. **Give** the **four participles** for each of these verbs:

	Active	Passive	Active	Passive
Pres.	_____		_____	
Perf.		_____		_____
Fut.	_____	_____	_____	_____

III. **Give** the **three infinitives** for each of these verbs:

Pres.	_____	_____
Perf.	_____	_____
Fut.	_____	_____

IV. The **imperative** forms of a **deponent verb** are similar to the forms for the present passive second person singular with the **alternate -re ending** and the regular second person plural. Give the **imperatives** for these **deponent verbs**:

	Singular	Plural
1. mīror	_____	_____
2. tueor	_____	_____
3. ēgredior	_____	_____
4. potior	_____	_____
5. orior	_____	_____
6. nascor	_____	_____

84

V. A. **Translate** these **direct questions into Latin:**

    e.g. 1. Who is Helen?   Quis est Helena?

          2. Where does Helen live?   Ubi_____ ?

          3. Why must Helen go with him?   Cūr_____dēbet?

          4. How must he carry off Helen?   Quōmodō_____dēbet?

    B. **Change** the **direct questions** above into **indirect questions (see LvO, 319-20)**

       introduced by "Paris knows ...." <u>Paris</u> <u>scit</u> ....:

e.g.   1. Paris scit quis Helena sit.

        Paris knows who Helen is.

      2. Paris scit ubi Helena _____.

        _____.

      3. Paris scit cūr _____.

        _____.

      4. Paris scit quōmodō_____.

        _____.

THE INDIRECT QUESTIONS ABOVE ARE ALL IN **PRIMARY SEQUENCE** (**LvO**, 261-62, 319-20).

VI. A. **Note** the translation of the **direct questions** with verbs in the **indicative:**

      1. Who was the king?   Quis erat rēx?

      2. Where was the war?   Ubi erat bellum?

      3. Why did we have to fight?   Cūr pugnāre dēbuimus?

      4. How did Odysseus travel?   Quōmodō Odysseus nāvigāvit?

B. **Change** the **questions** above into **indirect questions in secondary sequence**

      (see **LvO**, 320) introduced by "The Greeks asked ...." <u>Graecī</u> <u>rogāvērunt</u> ....":

e.g. 1. Graecī rogāvērunt quis rēx esset.

       The Greeks asked who the king was.

      2. Graecī rogāvērunt _____.

       _____.

      3. Graecī rogāvērunt _____.

       _____.

      4. Graecī rogāvērunt _____.

       _____.

Chapter XXXIII

I. A. **Decline** the **personal pronoun (see <u>LvO</u>, 119) <u>is, ea, id:</u>**

	Singular			Plural		
Nom.	_____	_____	_____	_____	_____	_____
Gen.	_____	_____	_____	_____	_____	_____
Dat.	_____	_____	_____	_____	_____	_____
Acc.	_____	_____	_____	_____	_____	_____
Abl.	_____	_____	_____	_____	_____	_____

B. What change would be made in declining the **intensive pronoun**

(<u>LvO</u>, 334) <u>īdem, eadem, idem</u>?_____

_____

C. What **case endings** are different from those of <u>bonus, -a, -um</u>

endings for the **pronoun/adjectives** like <u>sōlus</u> and <u>tōtus</u>?

____ singular, ending in ____; ____ singular, ending in ____.

II. **Change** each **personal pronoun** to an **intensive** or **demonstrative**

pronoun and **translate** each giving emphasis to the differences in

meaning:

(<u>Paris</u>) 1. Eum in proeliō vīdī. Hunc, Illum, Eundem, Ipsum, Istud

(<u>Hecuba</u>) 2. Eī corpus dedimus. Huic, Illī, Eīdem, Ipsī, Istī

(<u>Birds</u>) 3. Eae in arbore sunt. Hae, Illae, Eaedem, Ipsae, Istae

(<u>Animal</u>) 4. Id ē silvā exit. Hoc, Illud, Idem, Ipsum, Istud

(<u>Bodies</u>) 5. Ea humārī dēbent. Haec, Illa, Eadem, Ipsa, Ista

III. A. **Give principal parts** for the **impersonal verb <u>licet</u> (<u>LvO</u>, 336).**

_____

B. **Translate**: You may inspect the book. (inspect=<u>inspicere</u>)

_____

C. **Explain** the abbreviation <u>viz.</u> or <u>vidēlicet</u> (<u>LvO</u>, 406):

_____

D. **Explain** the abbreviation <u>sc.</u> or <u>scīlicet</u> (<u>LvO</u>, 406):

_____

IV. **Translate** each of these questions **into English** giving the correct meaning

to the **interrogatives** <u>nōnne</u> **and** <u>num</u> and give the implied answer:

<u>Answer</u>

e.g. 1. Nōnne Ulixēs est sapientior quam Āiax?

Ulysses is wiser than Ajax, isn't he?   Yes

2. Nōnne Helena immortālis est?

_____   _____

3. Num Āiax sagax erat?

_____   _____

4. Nōnne Āiax erat fortior Ulixe?

_____   _____

5. Num Āiax audax ōrātor ad arcēs mittēbātur?

_____   _____

6. Num Āiax Helenam reposcēbat?

_____   _____

7. Nōnne Ulixēs erat melior ōrātor quam Āiax?

_____   _____

V. **Fill in** the blanks with the correct form of the **partitive genitive case**

   (see <u>LvO</u>, **92, 320**)

1. Graecī partem _____ poscunt.   (of the booty)

2. Āiax plūs _____ voluit.   (of the honor)

3. Nil (Nihil) _____ mē tangit.   (of death = no death)

4. Pars _____ est mihi.   (of the good fortune= <u>fortuna, -ae</u>, f.)

5. Multa mīlia _____ spectāvimus.   (of men)

THIS USAGE IS CALLED **PARTITIVE GENITIVE** OR **GENITIVE OF THE**

WHOLE.

I. **Fill in** the blanks with the correct **accusative case** form (see <u>LvO</u>, **333**):

1. Omnēs Graecī praeter Ulixem _____ advēnērunt.   (home)

2. Saepe poēta Horātius _____ ībat.   (to the country)

3. Putō _____ esse fortiōrem quam Āiācem.   (Ulysses)

4. Ulixēs in marī Mediterraneō _____ errāvit. (for ten years)

Chapter XXXIV

I. A. **How many names** were common for Roman men of the Republic and

Empire (see <u>LvO</u>,338-41 for A-E)? _____

B. In <u>Gaius Julius Caesar</u>, what is the first name called?

_____; the central name _____; the last name _____

C. What did the ending <u>-por</u> mean at the end of a slave's name? _____

D. How were women usually named? _____

E. What do the names mean: Leo_____; Rex_____; Dexter_____

Alma_____; Clara_____; Lucy_____

II. **Give** the pattern for the **four participles** for <u>vocō</u> and <u>mittō</u> (see <u>LvO</u>, 347-48):

<u>Active</u>		<u>Passive</u>	
Pres. vocāns	calling	XXXXXXXX	XXXXXXXXX
Perf. XXXXXXX	XXXXXXXXX	_____	_____
Fut. _____	_____	_____	_____

Pres mittēns	sending	XXXXXXXX	XXXXXXXXX
Perf. XXXXXXX	XXXXXXXXX	_____	_____
Fut. _____	_____	_____	_____

Name the **four participles**:   1._____

2._____

3._____

4._____

What is another name for the **4th participle (#4)**?_____

III. A. What part of speech is the **gerundive**? <u>verbal</u>_____

B. What part of speech is the **gerund**? <u>verbal</u>_____

C. **Translate** these sentences containing **future passive participles**

(gerundives <u>LvO</u>, 347):

1. Coquus dē cēnā <u>preparandā</u> cogitābat.

_____

2. Polyxēna <u>interficienda</u> ē sinū mātris rapta est.

_____

88

3. Hecuba filiam <u>occīdendam</u> plorāvit.

_____

4. Fēminae <u>auferendae</u> oscula terrae Trōiānae dedērunt.

_____

5. Putō dē litterīs* <u>scrībendīs</u>.

_____

*The plural <u>litterīs</u> often refers to a single letter sent to a person.

IV. The **gerundive** used with a form of <u>sum</u> makes a verb phrase
   called the **passive periphrastic (see <u>Lvo</u>, 347-48)**:

   A. What does **periphrastic** mean? _____

   B. **Translate into English** a **passive periphrasic** construction,
      such as <u>Īnsula</u> procul <u>videnda</u> <u>est</u>:

   _____

   C. **Rephrase** these sentences which use a form of <u>dēbeō</u>, ought, into
      sentences using the **passive periphrastic**. Use the **dative of agent**
      with the **passive periphrastic.**

e.g. 1. Dēbētis amīcōs monēre.   1. Amīcī vōbīs monendī sunt.
     2. Dēbēmus discere linguās.   2. _____
     3. Dēbet parentibus parēre.   3. _____
     4. Patriam servāre dēbēs.   4. _____
     5. Līberī canēs cūrāre dēbent. 5. _____
     6. Mātrēs cibum parāre dēbent. 6. _____
     7. Malōs (virōs) timēre dēbēmus. 7. _____
     8. Līberī vidērī nōn audīrī   8. _____
        dēbent.
     9. Animālia amāre dēbēmus.   9. _____
    10. Pater filiōs amāre dēbet. 10. _____

Chapter XXXV

I. **Give a synopsis** of <u>ferō, ferre, tulī, lātum</u> in the third person singular, active and passive, indicative and subjunctive, with its 4 participles, 2 imperatives, and 6 infinitives **(see <u>LvO</u>, 435-36)**:

	Indicative		Subjunctive		Participles	
	<u>Active</u>	<u>Passive</u>	<u>Active</u>	<u>Passive</u>	<u>Active</u>	<u>Passive</u>
Pres.	fert	fertur	ferat	ferātur	ferēns	
Imp.	_____	_____	_____	_____		
Fut.	_____	_____			_____	_____
Perf.	_____	_____	_____	_____		_____
PPerf.	_____	_____	_____	_____		
FPerf.	_____	_____				

Imperatives: Singular: _____   Plural: _____

Infinitives: <u>Active</u>   <u>Passive</u>

	Active	Passive
Pres.	_____	_____
Perf.	_____	_____
Fut.	_____	_____

II. A. **Give** the **synopsis** for <u>sum, esse, fuī, futūrum</u>: **(see <u>LVO</u>, 433-34)**

	Indicative	Subjunctive
Pres.	est	sit
Imp.	_____	_____
Fut.	_____	
Perf.	_____	_____
PPerf.	_____	_____
FPerf.	_____	
Infinitives: Pres.	_____	
Perf.	_____	
Fut.	_____	

B. **Give** the **synopsis** for <u>possum, posse, potuī</u>: **(see <u>LvO</u>, 433-34)**

	Indicative	Subjunctive
Pres.	potest	possit
Imp.	_____	_____
Fut.	_____	
Perf.	_____	_____
PPerf.	_____	_____
FPerf.	_____	
	_____	
	_____	
	_____	

III. Review of the **subjunctive** (see <u>LvO</u>, **437 for all subjunctives**):

A. **Translate** each example of **independent subjuntive usage (<u>LvO</u>, 437)**:

1. **Jussive or Hortatory**: Fortēs laudēmus! _____

2. **Deliberative**: Quid faciam? Quid dicam? _____

3. **Optative**: Utinam māter vīvat! _____

4. **Potential**: Nēmō dīcāt mē esse miserum. _____

B. **Translate** each example of **dependent subjunctive usage (<u>LvO</u>, 437)**:

1. **Purpose**: Artifex urnās colōribus pingit ut fābulas **nārret**.

   _____

2. **Result**: Polyphēmus erat tam crudēlis ut hominēs **dēvorāret**.

   _____

3. **Conditions**: a. Should-Would   b. Contrary-to-Fact

   a. Sī nautae saccum ventōrum **aperiant**, ventī **effugiant**.

   _____

   b. Nisi nautae saccum ventōrum **aperuissent**, ventī nōn

      effūgissent.

   _____

4. **Cum clauses**: a. Circumstantial   b. Causal   c. Concessive

   a. Cum Laestrygōnēs cēterās nāvēs **dēmitterent**, nāvis Ulixis

      sōla effūgit.

   _____

   b. Cum nāvis ad Sirēnēs **appropinquāret**, Ulixēs aurēs virōrum

      cērā clausit.

   _____

   c. Cum Scylla nunc mōnstrum **esset**, tamen ōlim virgo pulchra

      fuerat.

   _____

5. **Noun clause of desire**: Circē Ulixem rogābat ut sēcum **remanēret**.

_____

Ulixēs Circae persuasit ut virōs, nunc porcōs, in hominēs

iterum **transfōrmāret**.

_____

6. **Indirect question**: Pēnelopa mirāta est quis advena **esset**.

_____

Ulixēs scīvit quī procī **essent** et quid **agerent**.

_____

7. **Relative clauses**: a. Characteristic   b. Purpose

a. Pēnelopa nōn erat uxor quae infidēlis **esset**.

_____

b. Procī servōs mīserat quī Pēnelopam in convivium **invītārent**.

_____

8. **After verbs of fearing** with **ut** meaning "that ...not" and **ne**

meaning "that" or "lest."

a. Pēnelopa verita est ut Ulixēs domum **revenīret**.

_____

b. Pēnelopa verita est nē ā procō in mātrimōnium **dūcerētur**.

_____

9. **Attraction** (within indirect discourse or subordinate clause):

a. Ulixēs scīvit procōs quī in rēgiā **habitārent** esse malōs.

_____

b. Ulixēs fīlium rogāvit ut procōs quī in rēgiā **essent** occīdere iuvāret.

_____

10. **Dum** meaning "until" is used with the subjunctive:

Exspectāvit dum reliquae nāvēs **convenīrent**.

_____

Graecī exspectāvērunt dum ventī secundī ratēs **movērent**.

_____

Chapter XXXVI

I. Of the many ways to express purpose, the **purpose clause (see LvO, 370)** is often used. **Supply the missing subjunctive verb and translate** these sentences **into English**:

1. Aenēas socium mīsit ut Ascanium _____ (to lead back).

_____

2. Dīdō nuntiōs mīsit ut Aenēan (Greek acc.) _____ (to find).

_____

II. The **supine (see LvO, 370)**, formed like the **neuter of the perfect passive participle**, is also used to express purpose:

1. Lāokoōn dēcurrit Trōiānōs monitum.

_____

III. The same idea of purpose can be expressed by ad with the **gerund**:

1. Lāokoōn dēcurrit ad Trōiānōs monendum.

_____

(not the preferred Latin usage, when the **gerund has an object**)

IV. When the **gerund has an object**, the preferred Latin usage is ad with the **gerundive modifying the object**:

1. Lāokoōn dēcurrit ad Trōiānōs monendōs.

_____

V. Purpose is also expressed by using **causā** or **grātiā** + the genitive of the preceding **gerund or gerundive**:

1. Lāokoōn dēcurrit Trōiānōrum monendōrum causā. (gerundive)

_____

2. Lāokoōn dēcurrit Trōiānōs monendī grātiā.(not preferred)

_____

Trōianorum monendōrum grātiā (preferred)

VI. The **Relative clause** can be used to express purpose:

1. Lāokoōn filiōs mīsit quī Trōiānōs monērent.

_____.

VII. **Rewrite** the first two sentences from the preceding page in
   all the other possible ways that are described on that page:

A. Purpose Clause: 1. Aenēas socium mīsit ut Ascanium redūceret.

   Supine: _____

   Ad + Gerund: _____

   Ad + Gerundive: _____

   Causā + Gerund: _____ *

   (or Gerundive):

   Grātiā + Gerund: _____ *

   (or Gerundive):

   Relative Clause: _____

B. Purpose Clause: 2. Dīdō nuntiōs mīsit ut Aenēan invenīret.

   Supine: _____

   Ad + Gerund: _____

   Ad + Gerundive: _____

   Causā + Gerund: _____ *

   (or Gerundive):

   Grātiā + Gerund   _____ *

   (or Gerundive):

   Relative Clause: _____

*Causā and grātiā usually stand after the gerund or gerundive.

VIII. The three meals **(see LvO, 359)** in the time of the Empire were:

   1. Breakfast _____

   2. Lunch   _____

   3. Dinner _____ which replaced the vesperna.

Chapter XXXVII

I. The **ablative case (see <u>LvO</u>, 349-50, 378)** is used for many expressions in Latin. The most common usage is with ideas of **means**, **agent**, **accompaniment**, and **manner**. To these usages are added ideas of **location** in place and time, of **separation**, and the ablative of **comparison** when <u>quam</u> is omitted. **Choose** the correct **ablative cases** in the following sentences and **decide** whether or not a **preposition** is necessary:

1. Arcas mātrem _____ necātūrus est.   (with an arrow)

    a) sagittīs   b) ā sagittā   c) sagittā   d) cum sagittā

2. Iuppiter _____ Mercuriō in terrā ambulat. (with his son)

    a) cum filiō   b) filiō   c) filiī   d) cum filiīs

3. Graecus Achaemenidēs _____ salvātus est.   (by a Trojan)

    a) Trōiānō   b) ā Trōiānō   c) cum Trōiānō   d) cum Trōiānīs

4. Tēlum _____ tormentī actum est.

    a) vī   b) vīs   c) ā vī   d) vim

5. Bracchia gigantis foedāta _____ erant.   (with gore)

    a) tābum   b) cum tābīs   c) tābō   d) tābī

6. Tū es cārior mihi _____.   (than life)

    a) vītā   b) quam vītam   c) vītae   d) vīta

    What other correct way to express this idea is possible?

    _____

7. Hī librī sunt meliōrēs _____.   (than those)

    a) illīs   b) quam illīs   c) illae   d) illōrum

    What other correct way to express this idea is possible?

    _____

8. _____ suōs domūs dēfendunt.   (with great care)

    a) cum cūrīs   b) cum magnō cūrō   c) magnā cum cūrā   d) cūrā magnā

9. Aeolus _____ rēgnat.   (on the Italian sea)

    a) Ītalicum profundum b) Ītalicī profundī c) Ītalicīs profundīs d) Ītalicō profundō

10. Mīlitēs praeda _____ cēlāvit.   (in the woods)

    a) in silvae   b) silvae   c) in silvā   d) in silvam

II. **Underline** the correct answer (see <u>LvO</u>, 378) in these choices for
translation (if more than one answer is correct, underline both):

1. We live <u>on an island smaller than Sicily.</u>

   a) in īnsulā minōre quam Siciliā.

   b) in īnsulā minōre quam Siciliam.

   c) in īnsulā minōre Siciliā.

   d) in īnsulā minōre Sicilia.

2. He spoke to us <u>more kindly</u> than to you.

   a) benignē b) benignius c) plus benignus d) benignissimē

3. The sun <u>rose</u> at at 7:00 A.M.

   a) oritur   b) ortus est   c) oriebatur   d) oriētur

4. We saw the students <u>playing</u> in the hall.

   a) lūdēns   b) lūdere   c) lūdentes   d) lusī

5. I do not wish you to suffer.

   a) patere   b) patī   c) passus es   d) passī estis

6. We <u>who are about to die</u> salute you.

   a) morī   b) mortuī sunt   c) moritūrī   d) moritūrōs

7. We gave the money to the women <u>seeking</u> help.

   a) petentis   b) petentibus   c) petentēs   d) petentī

8. <u>After the army had been defeated</u>, the Romans appointed a dictator.

   a) Exercitū victō b) Exercituī victō c) Exercitibus victīs d) Exercitum victum

9. The students, <u>who had been taught well</u>, gave a fine speech.

   a) bene doctōs b) bene docta c) bene doctī d) bene doctus

10. <u>We all ought to love our country.</u>

   a) Nōs omnēs patriam amāre dēbēmus.

   b) Nōbīs omnibus patriam amāre dēbēmus.

   c) Patria nōbīs omnibus amanda est.

11. Cato often declared, "<u>Carthage must be destroyed.</u>"

   a) Carthāgō dēlendō est.

   b) Carthāgā dēlenda est.

   c) Carthāginem dēlēre dēbēmus.

   d) Carthāgō dēlenda est.

Chapter XXXVIII

I. A. Name these **rooms (see <u>LvO</u>, 381)** in the **Roman house**:

    1. the entrance hall   _____

    2. the large reception hall   _____

    3. the bedrooms   _____

    4. the "wings"   _____

    5. the hole in the roof to admit   _____

       light, air, and rain to the atrium   _____

    6. the pool in the atrium   _____

    7. the master's study   _____

    8. the dining room   _____

    9. the toilet room   _____

  10. the kitchen   _____

  11. the garden surrounded by porticos   _____

       of colonnades

B. 1. What is the name for a Roman apartment building? _____

   2. Why does it have this name?

II. **Supply** the **object** in the **correct case (see <u>LvO</u>, 378-79)** following the **verbs of remembering and forgetting** in the sentences below:

    1. _____ semper meminimus.

       (Good friends)

    2. Nōlīte oblīviscī _____.

               (my birthday = diēs natālis)

    3. Oblītus es _____ quae didicistī.

        (all the things = use the neuter plural of omnis)

    4. Nōlī oblīviscī _____ prō līberīs.

        (the clothing = use plural)

    5. Kal. Iān. **(<u>LvO</u>, 439)** _____ meminisse dēbētis.

        (the gods)

III. **Label** each of the underlined words either **gerund** or **gerundive** (see <u>LvO</u>, 390-91) and **translate** the sentence **into Enlish**:

1. Medicus artī <u>sānandī</u> studet. (<u>sānāre</u>=to heal) _____

_____

2. Nōs dēvōvimus ad Graeciam <u>visitandam</u>. _____

_____

3. Poētae sunt perītī (perītae) in arte <u>scrībendī</u>. _____

_____

4. Tū tē dedistī ad mūsicam <u>discendam.</u> _____

_____

5. Fīlia mea sē dedit <u>docendō.</u> _____

_____

6. Fīlius tuus sē dedit ad fortūnam <u>quaerendam.</u> _____

_____

7. Discētis natāre <u>natandō.</u> _____

_____

IV. **Match** these characters **(see <u>LvO</u>, 385-87)** out of the <u>Odyssey</u>:

1. barbarian king who ate Ulysses' men   __ Polyphemus

2. changed Ulysses men to swine   __ Nereids

3. gave Ulysses moly as protection   __ Mercury

4. drank too much wine   __ Antiphates

5. the only one who did not drink the   __ Ulysses

6. saved by Aeneas from Polyphemus' island __ Circe

7. the Cyclops who was blinded by   __ Elpenor

8. the cannibals led by Antiphates   __ Eurylochus

9. helped Circe sorting out the herbs   __ Laestrygonians

10. blinded the Cyclops   __ Achaemenides

Chapter XXXIX

I. What is **deponent (see LvO, 403-05)** about a **deponent verb**?

_____

II. **How many tenses** are there for deponent verbs in the **indicative**?

____ **Name** them:_____, _____, _____, _____, _____, _____

III. **How many moods** are there for deponent verbs? _____ **Name**

them:_____, _____, _____, _____

IV. A. **List** the **main vowels** used in present tense in the **indicative mood:**

I   II   III   III-io   IV

____   ____   ____   ____   ____

B. **List** the **main vowels** for present tense in **subjunctive** mood?

____   ____   ____   ____   ____

V. What is the rule for the formation of the **imperfect subjunctive**?

_____ + _____

VI. **How many participles** are there for a **deponent verb**? _____

Give the **participles** for cōnor and sequor:

Pres.   _____   _____

Perf.   _____   _____

Fut.Act.   _____   _____

Fut.Pass.   _____   _____

VII. **How many infinitives** are there for a **deponent verb**? _____

Give the **infinitives** for the same verbs above:

Pres. _____   _____

Perf. _____   _____

Fut. _____   _____

VIII. **Form** the **imperatives**, singular and plural, for each of the

verbs above:

Singular   Plural   Singular   Plural

_____   _____   _____   _____

IX. **Give a synopsis** in second person singular for <u>conor</u> and second
person plural for <u>sequor</u>, indicative and subjunctive:

	Indicative	Subjunctive	Indicative	Subjunctive
Pres.	_____	_____	_____	_____
Imp.	_____	_____	_____	_____
Fut.	_____		_____	
Perf.	_____	_____	_____	_____
PPerf.	_____	_____	_____	_____
FPerf.	_____		_____	

X. **Translate** each verb in one way **into English**:

1. verentur _____ 6. sequerētur _____

2. loquēbantur _____ 7. mīrāns _____

3. potiēminī _____ 8. locūtūrus _____

4. mīrāta sum _____ 9. sī potīrer _____

5. sequātur _____ 10. sī potītus essem _____

XI. **Write** the **noun** in the **vocative case (see <u>LvO</u>, 403)** in the blanks:

1. Depōne metum, _____. (O, Trojan)

2. Disce, _____, mea verba. (wife)

3. Venīte, _____, in templum. (priests)

4. _____, magna petis. (O, greatest hero)

5. Scrībe, _____, litterās mihi hodiē. (mother)

6. _____, ignoscite mihi! (O, gods)

7. Vīve fēlīciter, _____ _____. (my son)

8. Vīvite magnō cum gaudiō, _____. (my daughters)

9. _____, respondēte mea verba verbīs vestrīs. (O, parents)

10. Audīte, _____, et cognoscētis. (my children)

11. Nōlī sedēre, _____, in hōc locō. (my friend)

12. Nōlīte scrībere, _____, in murōs. (children)

13. _____, ī ad formīcam et eius viās disce. (lazy one)

   (<u>lazy</u> = piger; used as a substantive) (formīca = <u>ant</u>)

Chapter XL

I. **Fill in** the blanks with the proper forms in the **dative case (see LvO, 412-14 for all dative exercises)**:

1. Multī nōn iam _____ crēdunt. (many gods)
2. Parentēs _____ ignoscere dēbent. (their children)
3. Dūcēs _____ imperāre oportet. (their soldiers)
4. Nōlīte nocēre _____. (your friends)
5. Semper parēte _____, līberī! (your parents)
6. Parce _____ et puerum indulgē nimis. (rod = ferula)
7. Magistra _____ persuāsit ut diligenter studērent. (her students)
8. Discipulī statim _____ respondērunt. (to their teacher)
9. Nōs omnēs _____ _____ servīmus. (to a good master)
10. Poētae _____ fābulārum nārrandārum student (to the art)
11. _____ placet scrībere tibi. (to me)

II. **Translate into Latin:**

1. I will trust him. _____
2. Forgive me, father. _____
3. Do not harm (Pl) them! _____
4. Spare (Sing) the women! _____
5. Obey (Sing) the judges. _____
6. He will persuade the judge. _____
7. They please the king. _____
8. I serve no master _____
9. We are studying new things. _____
10. Command me and I will obey. _____

III. **Fill in** the blanks with the proper **dative case** of the noun:

A. Dative with **indirect object**:

1. "Sīs mītissimus _____, pater." (to my son)
2. "Redde corpus meum _____." (to my parents)

B. Dative with **certain adjectives**:

   1. Venus semper fuit _____ cāra.

             (to her father Jupiter)

   2. Aenēas _____ grātus est.

        (to his mother)

   3. Estōte benignī _____. (Estōte is Fut. Imp. Pl.)

        (to animals)   **(see LvO, 435)**

C. Dative of **possession** with sum:

   1. Fortitūdō _____ erat.

        (to the soldiers)

   2. Sapientia _____ nōn erat.

        (to you)

D. Dative of **agent** with the **passive periphrastic**:

   1. Misericordia _____ petenda est.

        (by Turnus)

   2. Auxilium Evandrī _____ _____ quaerendum est.

        (by the Trojan Aeneas)

E. Dative of **reference**:

   1. Anchīsēs tālis genitor _____ fuit.

        (to you)

   2. _____ māter semper es, etiamsī nōn fīlius sim.

      (To me)

F. **Double dative**:

   1. Hoc aurum erit _____ _____.

        (as an aid)   (for the hero)

G. Dative with **compound verbs**:

   1. Imperātor _____ praefuit.

        (the soldiers)

102

oooooooo Key for Chapter I oooooooo

I. terra   terrae
    terram   terrās
    terrā   terrīs

II. 1. puellās   6. bonās fābulas
    2. rēgīnīs   7. parvās insulās
    3. chartae   8. rēgīnis pulchrīs
    4. paenīnsulas   9. in fābulīs prīmīs
    5. terrīs pulchrīs 10. bonae terrae

III. 1. habitant   they live
     2. rēgnant   they rule
     3. sunt   they are
     4. spectant   they look at

IV. 1. rēgnat   he, she, or it rules
    2. est   he, she, or it is
    3. habitat   he, she, or it lives
    4. spectat   he, she, or it looks at

V. 1. (The) good queens rule large lands.
    2. (The) beautiful girls live on the small islands.
    3. Where are the large islands?
    4. On the map the islands are large, but the peninsulas are small.
    5. They rule the large, beautiful lands.
    6. Europa lives in Phoenicia.
    7. Dido is the queen in the land (of) Africa.
    8. Dido lives and rules in Africa.

VI. 1. Charta nōn est magna; est parva.
    2. Terrae nōn sunt parvae; sunt magnae.
    3. Terrae sunt in Eurōpā, in Āfricā, in Asiā.
    4. Hispānia est in Eurōpā.
    5. Italia est in Eurōpā.
    6. Sicilia est in marī Mediterraneō.
    7. Ita, Graecia est in Eurōpā.
    8. Carthāgō est in Āfricā.
    9. Dīdō in Eurōpā nōn habitat; in Phoenīcā habitat.
    10. Āfrica nōn est terra parva; est terra magna.

VII. 1. Rēgīnae terrās rēgnant.   3. Puellae terrās spectant.
     2. Puella fābulās amat.   4. Rēgīna insulam rēgnat.
     The above are only four of many possibilities.

ᵒᵒᵒᵒᵒᵒᵒᵒ Key for Chapter II ᵒᵒᵒᵒᵒᵒᵒᵒ

I. A. possession
    B. the boy's home   the boys' home
       the girl's home   the girls' home
    C. the home **of the boy**   the home **of the boys**
       the home **of the girl**   the home **of the girls**
    D. puellae, of the girl   puellārum, of the girls
       rēginae, of the queen   rēginārum, of the queens

II. 1. bonās fīliās   10. bonās rēgīnās
    2. puellārum timidārum   11. habitant
    3. cum bonīs amīcīs   12. magnae terrae
    4. in parvīs īnsulīs   13. ad terrās novās
    5. sunt   14. portant
    6. dē rēgīnis novīs   15. bonōs poētās*
    7. narrant   16. fugitant
    8. amīcae timidae   17. cum rēgīnīs pulchrīs
    9. ad paenīnsulās pulchrās 18. magnārum chartārum
    *These are male poets; female poets would be <u>bonās poētās</u>.

III. 1. The friends carry large maps into a strange land.
     2. The friends of the queen flee to the beautiful
        island with the timid girls.
     3. The poets tell stories about the island.
     4. Where are the daughters of the poet?
     5. The girlfriend of the poet is not good.
     6. The girls look at the daughters of the queen.
     7. The girlfriends of the queen look at the small islands.
     8. The daughters of the queen flee with the timid girls.
     9. Who is the queen of the islands?

IV. 1. Eurōpā in Phoenīcā habitat.
     2. Tyrus est in Phoenīcā.
     3. Taurus est Iuppiter.
     4. Agēnor est rēx Phoenīcius.
     5. Agēnor nōn est taurus.
     6. Ita, amīcae Eurōpae sunt timidae.
     7. Iuppiter in Olympō habitat.
     8. Ita, Eurōpa amīcās amat.
     9. Taurus cum Eurōpā ad īnsulam Crētam fugitat.
    10. Ita, deus Iuppiter Eurōpam amat.

V. 1. Dīdō in Phoenīcā habitat.
    2. Deus puellam in terram pulchram portat.
    3. Rēgīna terram rēgnat.
    4. Eurōpa īnsulam spectat.
    5. Puella in īnsulā habitat.

VI. <u>5. here</u> hīc; <u>6. thus</u> ita; <u>1. once</u> ōlim; <u>7. almost</u> paene;
    <u>2. but</u> sed; <u>3.for a long time</u> diū;   <u>4. now</u> nunc

°°°°°°°° Key for Chapter III °°°°°°°°

I. 1. bonae deae
    2. parvīs casīs
    3. incolae timidae
    4. magistrās perītās
    5. nymphīs pulchrīs
    6. magnārum pictūrārum
    7. in magnīs silvīs
    8. puellae superbae
    9. bonae vītae
   10. cum nymphīs perītīs

   11. spectant
   12. labōrant
   13. rēgnant
   14. sunt
   15. habitant
   16. amant
   17. docent
   18. salvēte
   19. valēte
   20. dant

II. 1. The goddess tells a story.
    2. The wisdom of the farmer is great.
    3. In the great forest live a farmer and a poet.
    4. While the farmer works, his daughter makes beautiful pictures.
    5. Because the students work well, the teacher likes the students.
    6. The poet tells the farmer a story about the gods.
   (or) The poet tells a story about the gods to the farmer.

III. 1. Minerva est dea sapientiae.
     2. Arachnē est puella perīta in lānā.
     3. Arachnē nōn est dea.
     4. Dea in terrā nōn habitat.
     5. Puella est perīta quod Minerva est magistra.
     6. Nymphae in silvā habitant.
     7. Ita, nymphae pictūrās puellae laudant.
     8. Ita, pictūrae puellae sunt pulchrae.
     9. Pictūrae sunt pulchrae quod Minerva est magistra (or) quod puella est perīta.
    10. Ita, superbia est perīculosa.

IV. art n   prep adj n   v   n   pro v adj n
    The offspring of this union was Minos, who gave his name

    prep art n   prep n
    to the kings of Crete.

I. spectō   respondeō
    spectās   respondēs
    spectat   respondet
    spectāmus   respondēmus
    spectātis   respondētis
    spectant   respondent

II.
1. est — he/she/it is
2. monstrō — I show, am showing, do show
3. ambulās — you walk, are walking, do walk
4. negā! — deny! (sing)
5. dēbet — he/she/it owes, is owing, does owe
6. doceō — I teach, am teaching, do teach
7. es — you are
8. vocō — call, am calling, do call
9. simulā! — pretend!
10. certat — he/she/it strives, is striving, does strive
11. habēs — you have, are having, do have
12. clāmat — he/she/it shouts, is shouting, does shout
13. sum — I am
14. salvē — be well!, hello!
15. fōrmās — you make, are making, do make
16. dēsīderō — I want, am wanting, do want
17. rēgnā bene! — rule well!
18. portat — he/she/it carries, is carrying, does carry
19. narrās — you tell, are telling, do tell
20. respondet — he/she/it replies, is replying, does reply

III.
1. estis
2. sumus
3. esse
4. sum
5. est
6. estne?
7. negat
8. negāre
9. negant
10. negāsne? negātisne?

IV.
1. fēminae
2. discipulīs
3. ad casam
4. fīliae
5. incolīs
6. ad īnsulam
7. fēminīs
8. mihi
9. ad silvās or silvam
10. ad bonam terram

V.
1. We ought to love a skillful teacher.
2. The teacher is trying to teach the students.
3. The timid women are trying to flee into the forest.
4. The lady wants to give a picture to the farmer.
5. While you (pl.) are walking in the woods, I am trying to work.
6. The goddess ought to give wisdom to students.
7. You ought to show my house to the farmer.
8. We are trying again to give wisdom to the farmers.
9. I do not desire to be with a foolish teacher.

VI.
1. Spectāte! — Look!
2. Respondēte! — Reply!
3. Clāmāte! — Shout!
4. Date! — Give!
5. Labōrāte! — Work!
6. Docēte! — Teach!
7. Laudāte! — Praise!
8. Salvēte! — Be well! Hello! Greetings!
9. Valēte! — Be strong! Be Well! Goodbye!
10. Certāte! — Struggle! Compete!

VII. amā-   ambulā-   respondē-   docē-

Drop the -re from the infinitive to form the stem (which is
also the same form as the imperative singular).

°°°°°°°° Key for Chapter V °°°°°°°°

I. 1. vocābāmus   we called, were calling, did call, used to call
    2. docēbat   he/she/it taught, was teaching, did teach, used to teach
    3. mūtābat   he/she/it changed, was changing, did change, used to change
    4. prohibēbam   I prevented, was preventing, did prevent, used to prevent
    5. necābātis   you killed, were killing, did kill, used to kill
    6. pendēbant   they hung, were hanging, did hang, used to hang
    7. amābās   you (sing.) loved, were loving, did love, used to love
    8. clāmābāmus   we shouted, were shouting, did shout, used to shout
    9. habitābat   he/she/it lived, was living, did live, used to live
    10. portābātis you (pl.) carried, were carrying, did carry, used to carry

II. 1. you (sing.) were   7. erāmus
    2. you (pl.) were   8. erant
    3. he/she/it was   9. erās
    4. I was   10. erātis
    5. we were   11. eram
    6. they were   12. erat

III. 1. puellae
     2. nymphīs
     3. Mihi
     4. tibi
     5. incolīs

IV. Imperative Mood

A. 1. Look!   2. Shout!   3. Hail!   4. Farewell!   5. Teach!
      Spectā!   Clāmā!   Salvē!   Valē!   Docē!

B. 1. agricola
   2. domina
   3. Minerva
   4. dea
   5. magistra, magister

V. 1. Minerva
   2. Arachnē
   3. puellae
   4. domina
   5. fēmina
   6. nymphae
   7. agricolae
   8. deae

Nationality Game

1. Britannica
2. Āfricāna
3. Germānica
4. Graeca
5. Italica
6. Hispāna or Hispānica

°°°°°°°° Key for Chapter VI °°°°°°°°

I.
duodecim	octō	quattuor
ūndecim	septem	trēs
decem	sex	duo
novem	quīnque	ūnus

II.
bonus puer	bonī puerī	templum sacrum	templa sacra
bonī puerī	bonōrum puerōrum	templī sacrī	templōrum sacrōrum
bonō puerō	bonīs puerīs	templō sacrō	templīs sacrīs
bonum puerum	bonōs puerōs	templum sacrum	templa sacra
bonō puerō	bonīs puerīs	templō sacrō	templīs sacrīs

III.
1. Pīrāta īrātus
2. Poētae perītī (perītae, if women poets)
3. Multōs agricolās
4. nautā temerāriō
5. poētārum clārōrum or clārārum, if women poets

IV. DLXXV
DCCLXXXIII
CMXCV or MCMCCCCV

V.
1. Why   2. Who   3. Where   4. What
5. The enclitic -ne attached to the first word is the sign that the sentence
   is a question.

VI.
diū	for a long time	hīc	here	ita	thus, so
ōlim	once upon a time	hūc	to this place	bene	well
nunc	now	ibi	there	certē	surely
saepe	often			maximē	especially
iterum	again			minimē	least
aeternō	eternally			optimē	very well
prīmō	first, at first			melius	better
deinde	then			paene	almost
dēnique	finally				

1. Saepe puerōs vocō.
2. Hīc habitō.
3. Optimē labōrō.
4. Aeternō discipulōs amō.
5. Prīmō deōs vocō.
6. Dēnique puerōs vocō.

These are only six sentences of many possible combinations.

°°°°°°°° Key for Chapter VII °°°°°°°°°

I. rēgia pulchra   equus meus   verbum ultimum
rēgiae pulchrae   equī meī   verbī ultimī
rēgiae pulchrae   equō meō   verbō ultimō
rēgiam pulchram   equum meum   verbum ultimum
rēgia pulchrā   equō meō   verbō ultimō

rēgiae pulchrae   equī meī   verba ultima
rēgiārum pulchrārum   equōrum meōrum   verbōrum ultimōrum
rēgiīs pulchrīs   equīs meīs   verbīs ultimīs
rēgiās pulchrās   equōs meōs   verba ultima
rēgiīs pulchrīs   equīs meīs   verbīs ultimīs

II. 1. convocābant   they were calling together
2. exercēmus   we are exercising
3. honōrātis   you are honoring
4. iuvābant   they were helping
5. lacrimātis   you are crying
6. stāmus   we are standing
7. rogābant   they were asking
8. volābātis   you were flying
9. circumspectābāmus   we were looking around
10. monēbantne...?   did they warn...?

III. 1. sagittīs   2. lacrimīs   3. ālīs   4. verbīs suīs   5. oculīs superbīs

IV. 1. How many horses are in the field? Seven.
2. How many mothers are standing in the temple? Four.
3. How many arrows do you have? Five.
4. How many sons do you have? Three.
5. How many daughters do you have? Three.
6. How many children do you have? Six.
7. How many funerals did Niobe have? Fourteen.
8. How many fingers do you have? Ten.
9. How many eyes do you have? Two.
10. How many gods have the Romans? Many, but twelve great gods.

°°°°°°° Key for Chapter VIII °°°°°°°°°

I. portābō portābimus   monēbō monēbimus
portābis portābitis   monēbis monēbitis
portābit portābunt   monēbit monēbunt

II. 1. bonōrum puerōrum   6. multās undās
2. virī optimī   7. virī miserī
3. nullum auxilium   8. bracchiōrum meōrum
4. in rīpā umbrōsā   9. ultimus sonus
5. agrī plānī   10. virō optimō

III. 1. puerōs miserōs   6. papyrōs densōs
2. auxilium nullum   7. satyrum miserum
3. bracchium tuum   8. sonum nullum
4. concilia digna   9. virōs cēterōs
5. fugam ultimam   10. deōs magnōs

IV. 1. vocābit   Pan will call Syrinx.
    2. vidēbit   Syrinx will see the satyr.
    3. amābunt   Satyrs will love nymphs.
    4. fugitābit   The nymph will flee across the fields.
    5. transfōrmābunt   The nymphs will change Syrinx.
    6. habēbō   I shall have no help.
    7. habēbimus   We shall not have good fields.
    8. Eritne   Will the sound be great?
    9. Habēbisne   Will you have no words?
    10. habēbō   I shall not have tears (I shall not cry).

V. 1. Ita, Pān Syringam aeternō amābit.
    2. Syringa sē Diānae dēvovēbit.
    3. Nullus vir, nullus deus Syringam habēbit.
    4. Papyrōs in bracchiīs Pān tenēbit.
    5. Nymphae Syringam in papyrōs transfōrmābunt.

VI. 1. they will be   2. we shall be   3. I shall be
    4. you (pl.) will be   5. you (sing. will be   6. he/she/it will be

°°°°°°° Key for Chapter IX °°°°°°°°°

I.

portāvī	I have carried*	docuī	I have taught*
portāvistī	you have carried	docuistī	you have taught
portāvit	he has carried	docuit	she has taught
portāvimus	we have carried	docuimus	we have taught
portāvistis	you have carried	docuistis	you have taught
portāvērunt	they have carried	docuērunt	they have taught

*The simple "I carried" and "I taught" and the emphatic "did carry" and "did teach" are possible English translations for each form.

II. 1. vīdit   6. dedistis
    2. narrāvimus   7. stetī
    3. narrābant   8. stābam
    4. amāvistī   9. iūvēruntne
    5. vocābat   10. habuimus

III. 1. deō   2. deō   3. deō   4. deō   5. mihi   6. Italiae

IV. 1. vidēbit ...,   erit   5. cūrābis ...,   dabunt
    2. docēbis ...,   erimus   6. cūrābimus ...,   erunt
    3. iacēbō ...,   vidēbō   7. cūrābit ...,   dabit
    4. invocābō ...,   respondēbunt

V. 1. suōs   Parents ought to love their (own) sons.
    2. eius   Marcus does not like her clothes.
    3. eius   A pin held back her garments.
    4. sua   The women held their garments together with pins.
    5. suam   Arcas almost killed his own mother.
    6. eius   Arachne did not like her (Minerva's) pictures.
    7. suās   Arachne liked her own pictures.

VI. Indicate your Zodiac sign; describe its characteristics and your own. Look up the signs and months in **LvO**, 77.

°°°°°°° Key for Chapter X °°°°°°°°°

I. dedī   I have given, gave, did give   vīdī   I have seen, saw, did see
    dedistī   you have given, gave, did give   vīdistī   you have given, saw, did see
    dedit   he has given, gave, did give   vīdit   he/she/it has seen, saw, did see
    dedimus   we have given, gave, did give   vidimus   we have seen, saw, did see
    dedistis you have given, gave, did give   vīdistis you have seen, saw, did see
    dedērunt they have given, gave, did give   vidērunt they have seen, saw, did see

II. 1. they have remained   5. adfuit
    2. you (s.) have saved   6. fugitāvī
    3. I have stretched, extended 7. exspectābāmus
    4. we have carried   8. exspectāvimus

III. 1. dedimus 2. stābant 3. temptābat 4. mansērunt

IV. A. 1. vidēre   6. exspectāvī
        2. mansī   7. dedī
        3. fugitāvī   8. stāre
        4. absum   9. habēre
        5. adesse   10. iūvī (N.B. irregular)
    B. Infinitive gives present stem
    C. 3rd principal part gives perfect stem.

V.   1. tredecim   2. sēdecim   3. quīndecim
VI. fuī   fuistī   fuit   fuimus   fuistis   fuērunt

°°°°°°°° Key for Chapter XI °°°°°°°°°

I. A. alma māter   almae mātrēs
       almae mātris   almārum mātrum
       almae mātrī   almīs mātribus
       almam mātrem   almās mātrēs
       almā mātre   almis matribus
   B. the school from which one has graduated, the school which
      nourished the student in his/her tender years.

II. rēgia   regal
    rēgnāre   regicide
    rēgīna   Elizabeth Regina
III. A. thousand; B. milligram, millimeter, millennium, etc.; C. one thousandth of a dollar or
        one-tenth of a cent; D. mīlia; E. mile
IV. A. genitive plural; B. finium & partium; C. I-stem nouns of the 3rd declension

V. 1. partēs ultimae   the last parts   VI. 1. Duae   4. duās
    2. patrum nostrōrum   of our fathers   2. duārum   5. duābus
    3. bonīs rēgibus   to/for good kings   3. duābus   6. duōs
    4. piscēs immensōs   huge fish
    5. senum piōrum   of pious old men
    6. membra longa   long limbs
    7. mensīs plānīs   (on) level tables
    8. arborēs umbrōsae   shady trees
    9. dominīs benignīs   to/for kind masters
   10. servīs miserīs   to/for wretched slaves

°°°°°°° Key for Chapter XII °°°°°°°°°

I. nōmen fāmōsum   nōmina fāmōsa
    nōminis fāmōsī   nōminum fāmōsōrum
    nōminī fāmōsō   nōminibus fāmōsīs
    nōmen fāmōsum   nōmina fāmōsa
    nōmine fāmōsō   nōminibus fāmōsīs

II. 1. Videō puerōs bene vīvere.
     2. Videō servōs bracchia tendere.
     3. Videō mātrēs fābulās dē fīliābus narrāre.
     4. Videō senēs ānserem prehendere.
     5. Videō hominēs optimē vīvere.

III. 1. Malōs 2. Bona 3. Multōs 4. Multa 5. Piī

IV. 1. vastō   vastāre (1)   vastāvī   vastātum   destroy
     2. vīvō   vīvere   (3)   vīxī   victum   conquer
     3. timeō   timēre   (2)   timuī   XXXXXX   fear
     4. dubitō   dubitāre (1)   dubitāvī   dubitātum doubt
     5. iubeō   iubēre   (2)   iussī   iussum   order
     6. parō   parāre   (1)   parāvī   parātum   prepare
     7. sedeō   sedēre   (2)   sēdī   sessum   sit

V. 1. Nōlī terrās vastāre.   Nōlīte terrās vastāre.
    2. Nōlī male vīvere.   Nōlīte male vīvere.
    3. Nōlī deōs timēre.   Nōlīte deōs timēre.
    4. Nōlī deōs dubitāre.   Nōlīte deōs dubitāre.
    5. Nōlī puerōs iubēre.   Nōlīte puerōs iubēre.
    6. Nōlī cēnam parāre.   Nōlīte cēnam parāre.
    7. Nōlī in templō sedēre.   Nōlīte in templō sedēre.

VI. vastāverat; vīxerat; timuerat; dubitāverat; iusserat; parāverat; sēderat.

°°°°°°°° Key for Chapter XIII °°°°°°°°

I. nox clārissima   noctēs clārissimae
    noctis clārissimae   noctium clārissimārum
    noctī clārissimae   noctibus clārissimīs
    noctem clārissimam   noctēs clārissimās
    nocte clārissimā   noctibus clārissimīs

II. 1. grātissimus   6. altissimus
     2. nōtissimum   7. maxima
     3. clārissimus   8. raucissima
     4. grātissima   9. cārissima
     5. fōrmōsissimus, or -a*   10. fōrmōsissimum
*iuvenis can be either masculine or feminine (common gender).

III. amāverō   iusserō
      amāveris   iusseris
      amāverit   iusserit
      amāverimus   iusserimus
      amāveritis   iusseritis
      amāverint   iusserint

IV. 1. possum   6. potēs
     2. possumus   7. possum
     3. potest   8. possunt
     4. potestis   9. potest
     5. potest   10. potest

V. 1. dolō   2. testā   3. patre Iove   4. albīs foliīs

VI. A. 1. Whom did Echo love?
       2. Whom did Jupiter save?
       3. Whom did Arachne call?
   B. 1. The youth whom Echo loved was Narcissus.
       2. The youth whom Jupiter saved was Arcas.
       3. The goddess whom Arachne called was Minerva.

°°°°°°°°° Key for Chapter XIV °°°°°°°°°

I.

dūcō	dūcēbam	dūxī	dūxeram	dūxerō
dūcis	dūcēbās	dūxistī	dūxerās	dūxeris
dūcit	dūcēbat	dūxit	dūxerat	dūxerit
dūcimus	dūcēbāmus	dūximus	dūxerāmus	dūxerimus
dūcitis	dūcēbātis	dūxistis	dūxerātis	dūxeritis
dūcunt	dūcēbant	dūxērunt	dūxerant	dūxerint

II.

faciō	faciēbam	fēcī	fēceram	fēcerō
facis	faciēbās	fēcistī	fēcerās	fēceris
facit	faciēbat	fēcit	fēcerat	fēcerit
facimus	faciēbāmus	fēcimus	fēcerāmus	fēcerimus
facitis	faciēbātis	fēcistis	fēcerātis	fēceritis
faciunt	faciēbant	fēcērunt	fēcerant	fēcerint

III. 1. Ego ... tū   I love you, but you do not love me.
     2. Nōbīs   They gave gifts to us.
     3. Eīs   Tell them a story, please.
     4. Nōs   We like the poet's stories.
     5. vōbīscum   The Lord be with you.

IV. A. Fill in the blanks in the drawing:
     B. 1. caput, capitis   15. nāsus, -ī
        2. faciēs, faciētis   16. dens, dentis
        3. collus, -ī   17. supercilia, -ae
        4. cor, cordis   18. lingua, -ae
        5. cor, cordis   19. abdōmen, -inis
        6. digitus, -ī   20. digitus, -ī
        7. abdōmen, -inis   21. genū + flectere
        8. pēs, pedis   22. manus, -ūs
        9. capillus, -ī   23. pectus, pectoris
      10. cerebrum, ī   24. bracchium, -iī
      11. frons, frontis   25. musculus, -ī
      12. oculus, -ī   26. truncus, -ī
      13. auris, auris   27. membrum, -ī
      14. ōs, oris   28. corpus, corporis

IV. A. PARTES CORPORIS

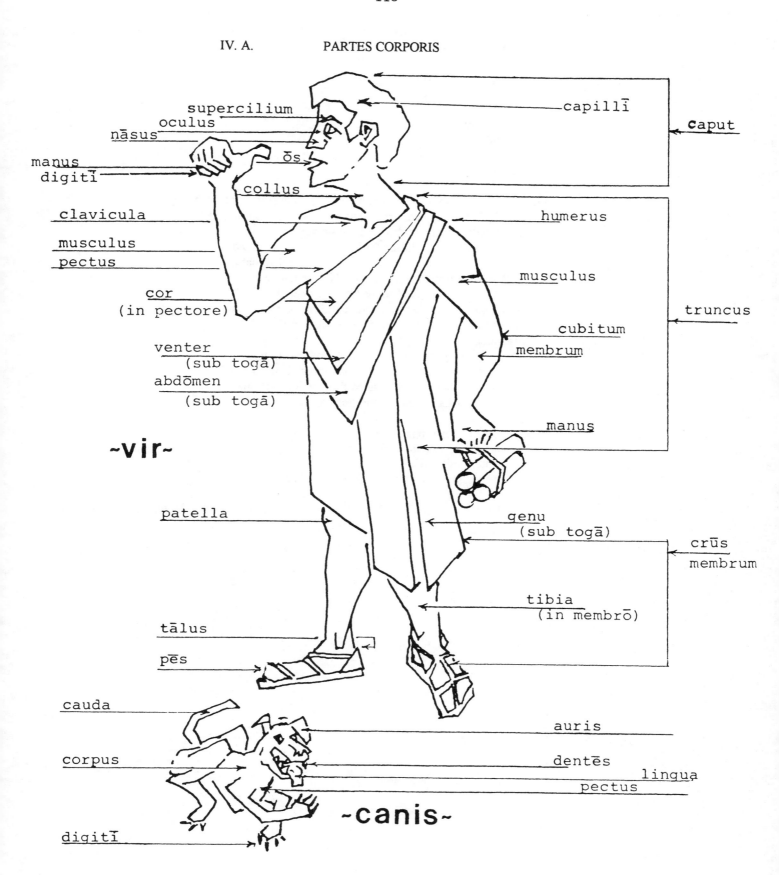

supercilium
oculus
nāsus
capillī
caput

manus
digitī
ōs
collus

clavicula
humerus

musculus
pectus
musculus

cor
(in pectore)
cubitum
membrum

venter
(sub togā)
abdōmen
(sub togā)
manus

truncus

~vir~

patella
genu
(sub togā)

crūs
membrum

tibia
(in membrō)

tālus
pēs

cauda
auris

corpus
dentēs
lingua
pectus

~canis~

digitī

V. 1. corpore   bracchia
    2. bracchiō/bracchiīs
    3. digitōs
    4. digitōs   pedibus
    5. capite   capillī
    6. crūra
    7. ventrum
    8. dentibus
    9. oculīs
   10. pedibus

VI. A. "The human body has many limbs, among which are the hands,
        mouth, teeth, stomach, legs. Once the rest of the parts
        of the body were angry because the stomach received
        everything but did nothing for itself. Then they agreed
        upon this plan among themselves. They decided that the
        teeth would chew no food, the hands would not carry any
        food to the mouth. And so the body was not able to be
        strong and the whole body died. Citizens, do not destroy
        our country in this same manner because of your
        discontent.
          "It is necessary for the human body to have all its parts;
        it is necessary for the country to have both patricians and
        plebians." The plebs understood the story of Menenius
        Agrippa and accepted the conditions for peace.

    B. 1. Menēnius Agrippa erat patricius.
        2. Partēs corporis sunt caput, manūs, ōs, dentēs, venter.
        3. Venter nihil sibi ēgit.
        4. Ita, necesse est corpus humanum omnēs partēs habēre.

Parts of the Body: ANSWERS TO CROSSWORD PUZZLES AT END OF KEY, PAGE 140

°°°°°°° Key for Chapter XV °°°°°°°

I.
vocābō	manēbō	dūcam	capiam	sentiam
vocābis	manēbis	dūcēs	capiēs	sentiēs
vocābit	manēbit	dūcet	capiet	sentiet
vocābimus	manēbimus	dūcēmus	capiēmus	sentiēmus
vocābitis	manēbitis	dūcētis	capiētis	sentiētis
vocābunt	manēbunt	dūcent	capient	sentient

II.
vocō	manēs	dūcit	capimus	sentiunt
vocābam	manēbās	dūcēbat	capiēbāmus	sentiēbant
vocābō	manēbis	dūcet	capiēmus	sentient
vocāvī	mansistī	dūxit	cēpimus	sēnsērunt
vocāveram	manserās	dūxerat	cēperāmus	sēnserant
vocāverō	manseris	dūxerit	cēperimus	sēnserint

III. 1. pulcherrima 2. miserrimus 3. sacerrimum

IV. 1. Although the men ought to remain near their houses, they are
      wandering through the towns.
   2. If your son is holding (will hold) a javelin in his hand, other children will see him.
   3. If I give (will give) no aid to the man, he will not be my friend.
   4. Will you indicate to me the price of the sword secretly?
   5. When I approached the town of the famous oracle, why did you avoid me?
   6. If you fly through the sky, the men will give you the greatest help.
   7. We remained in a dangerous town, but you hid near the river bank.
   8. Thisbe will flee if she sees (will see) the lion.
   9. The lovers have a plan: they will deceive their parents and leave their houses and
      meet at the tomb of Ninus.
   10. Pyramus also will seek death if he sees (will see) the bloody garment of Thisbe.

V. 1. sē 2. sē 3. sē 4. sē 5. eam 6. eōs or eās 7. suōs 8. eius 9. mē 10. eius

VI.
1. bibere	3 -e-	7. quaerere	3 -e-
2. convenīre	4 -ie-	8. dēbēre	2 -bi-
3. fallere	3 -e-	9. relinquere	3 -e-
4. fugere	3 -ie-	10. sentīre	4 -ie-
5. optāre	1 -bi-	11. manēre	2 -bi-
6. pervenīre	4 -ie-	12. venīre	4 -ie-

VII.
ex + abl.	ex oppidō
sub + acc. or abl.	sub undās/ sub undīs
ad + acc.	ad īnsulam
in + acc. or abl.	in silvam/ in silvā
dē + abl.	dē pōmīs
ab + abl.	ab itinere
prō + abl.	prō domū
cum + abl.	cum leōne
inter + acc.	inter amantēs
post + acc.	post mortem
propter + acc.	propter cruōrem
trans + acc.	trans parietem
per + acc.	per fissum
prope + acc.	prope arborem
praeter + acc.	praeter ducem

°°°°°°°° Key for Chapter XVI °°°°°°°°

I.
hic	haec	hoc	ille	illa	illud
huius	huius	huius	illīus	illīus	illīus
huic	huic	huic	illī	illī	illī
hunc	hanc	hoc	illum	illam	illud
hōc	hāc	hōc	illō	illā	illō

hī	hae	haec	illī	illae	illa
hōrum	hārum	hōrum	illōrum	illārum	illōrum
hīs	hīs	hīs	illīs	illīs	illīs
hōs	hās	haec	illōs	illās	illa
hīs	hīs	hīs	illīs	illīs	illīs

II.
hic leō	haec hōra	hoc consilium
huius leōnis	huius hōrae	huius consiliī
huic leōnī	huic hōrae	huic consiliō
hunc leōnem	hanc hōram	hoc consilium
hōc leōne	hāc hōrā	hōc consiliō

hī leōnēs	hae hōrae	haec consilia
hōrum leōnum	hārum hōrārum	hōrum consiliōrum
hīs leōnibus	hīs hōrīs	hīs consiliīs
hōs leōnēs	hās hōrās	haec consilia
his leōnibus	hīs hōrīs	hīs consiliīs

III. 1. illīus perīculī
2. illud monumentum
3. in illīs urnīs
4. illōrum comitum
5. illī amantī
6. illa pōma
7. illa tempora
8. illōrum gladiōrum
9. illīs consiliīs
10. in illō itinere

IV. 1. Amāte   2. Monēte   3. Petite   4. Capite   5. Sentīte

V. 1. legimus   4. lēgimus
2. legēbāmus   5. lēgerāmus
3. legēmus   6. lēgerimus

117

°°°°°°° Key for Chapter XVII °°°°°°°°

I. A. SING: I, you, he (she, it); PL: we, you, they

B. IMP: -bā-; 　　C. FUT: for 1st and 2nd: -bi- ; for 3rd & 4th: -ē-(-iē)

II. 1. I am called
2. you (sing.) were warned
3. he/she/it will be sought
4. we are made
5. we were made
6. they are felt
7. you (pl.) are called
8. you (sing.) are sought
9. he/she/it is made
10. you (pl.) are warned

III. 1. to whom　　dat. sing.
to which
2. about whom　abl. pl.
about which
3. whom/which masc. acc. pl.
4. who　fem. nom. sing.
who　fem. nom. pl.
which　neut. nom. pl.
which　neut. acc. pl.
5. to whom/which   acc. sing.
6. without which　abl. sing
without whom
7. with whom/which abl. pl.

8. whose/of whom gen. sing.
of which
9. after which　acc. sing.
after whom　acc. sing.

10. from/by whom fem. abl. sing.
from/by which fem. abl. sing.

11. to whom　　dat. pl.
to which
12. which　　nom. sing.
which　　acc. sing.
13. on account of which/
on which account　acc. sing.

14. who/which masc. nom. sing.
who/which　masc.nom. pl.
15. whom/which　masc.acc. sing.
16. whom/which　fem.acc. pl.

17. whose/of whom
of which　mas. gen. pl.
whose/of whom　neut. gen. pl.
18. through which　acc. pl.

19. whose/of whom　fem. gen. pl.
of which
20. by whom　masc. abl. sing.
by which　neut. abl. sing.

IV. 1. This youth is moved by the power of love.
2. The maiden Atalanta flees the lover whom she fears.
3. I was calling the woman who was condemned by them.
4. He avoided the danger which was feared by us.
5. The most beautiful goddess of love, who is adored by all, will help the youth.
6. Do those things which you ought to do.
7. I do not love this man who does not love others.
8. These men feared the king whose town was captured.
9. I do not know that man to whom aid was given.
10. These apples which were given by the goddess will help you.

V. 1. quae　3. cuius　5. quōs
2. quī　4. quī　6. quō

°°°°°°°° Key for Chapter XVIII °°°°°°°°

I. A. Perfect: having Passive: been Participle: seen
    B. adjective declined like <u>bonus, bona, bonum</u>
    C. 1. ductus, -a, -um   (having been) led
       2. adōrātus, -a, -um   (having been) adored
       3. carptus, -a, -um   (having been) picked
       4. parātus, -a, -um   (having been) prepared
       5. iactus, -a, -um   (having been) thrown
       6. prōmissus, -a, -um   (having been) promised
       7. scrīptus, -a, -um   (having been) written
       8. captus, -a, -um   (having been) captured

II. 1. ducta   3. carpta   5. iactīs   7. scrīptās   9. damnātō
    2. adōrātam   4. parātā   6. prōmissa 8. captae   10. mōtīs

III. A. it   he/she/it goes, is going , does go
         ībat   he/she/it went, was going, did go, used to go
         ībit   he/she/it will go
    (īvit)   iit   he/she/it has gone, went, did go
    (īverat) īerat   he/she/it had gone
    (īverit) īerit   he/she/it will have gone

     B. 1. adeō   3. exeō   5. subeō   7. transeō
        2. abeō   4. ineō   6. redeō   8. pereō

IV. quis   quid   quī   quae   quae
     cuius   cuius   quōrum   quārum   quōrum
     cui   cui   quibus   quibus   quibus
     quem   quid   quōs   quās   quae
     quō   quō   quibus   quibus   quibus

V. 1. Who is the goddess who is kind to lovers?
    2. Whose apples did Hippomenes throw in the race?
    3. To whom did Hippomenes not give thanks and not give gifts?
    4. Whom did Hippomenes, moved by love, desire to overcome?
    5. Moved by what, did Atalanta try to warn Hippomenes?
    6. O, Hippomenes, who has led you into these dangerous paths?
    7. By whom was Atalanta led into marriage?
    8. Whom did the goddess transform into lions?

VI. 1. I shall be influenced   11. you (sing.) have gone
    2. I am promised   12. I have demanded, demanded
    3. to be led   13. rejoice!
    4. you (pl.) go, are going, do go 14. I was going
    5. he will have thrown   15. to go
    6. they were rejoicing   16. I shall be adored
    7. they go   17. to be moved
    8. I have run, I ran   18. they will go
    9. they had gone   19. (having been) led
    10. you (pl.) are adored   20. he will demand

VII. 1. The men surpassed by Atalanta were killed.
  2. The enemy has killed the conquered men.
  3. The old man, warned by his friends, will flee to us.
  4. The captured man said nothing.
  5. Unless we (will have) help(ed) my captured father, he will be killed.
  6. I do not know the condemned woman.
  7. I could not find the book sent by you.
  8. I desire to hear about the things done by him.
  9. I shall give the promised aid to my mother.
  10. We ought to give many rewards to the wounded men.

°°°°°°°° Key for Chapter XIX °°°°°°°°

I.

A.
dīēs faustus	lucky day (SUBJ)	diēs faustī	lucky days
diēī faustī	of a lucky day	diērum faustōrum	of lucky days
diēī faustō	to/for a lucky day	diēbus faustīs	to/for lucky days
diem faustum	lucky day (DO)	diēs faustōs	lucky days
diē faustō	on a lucky day	diēbus faustīs	on lucky days

B.
dīēs fēlix	happy day (SUBJ	diēs fēlicēs	happy days
diēī fēlicis	of a happy day	diērum fēlicium	of happy days
diēī fēlicī	to/for a happy day	diēbus fēlicibus	to/for happy days
diem fēlicem	happy day (DO)	diēs fēlicēs	happy days
diē fēlicī	on a happy day	diēbus fēlicibus	on happy days

II.
omnis vir	every man (SUBJ)	omnēs virī	all men
omnis virī	of every man	omnium virōrum	of all men
omnī virō	to/for every man	omnibus virīs	to/for all men
omnem virum	every man (DO)	omnēs virōs	all men
ab omnī virō	by every man	ab omnibus virīs	by all men

There is an -i in almost all the singular forms of omnis, and an -i in the genitive plural: omnium (like finium and partium). Most third declension adjectives are considered I-stems.

III. 1. With the war having been ended,
    When the war had ended, / After the war was over,

  2. With the apple having been thrown,
    After the apple had been thrown / After he had thrown the apple,

  3. With the golden touch having been given,
    Because (When) he had been given the golden touch,

  4. With the food being golden,
    Because the food was now golden, / Since the food was golden,

  5. With the stone having been thrown,
    After the stone had been thrown,

  6. With these words having been heard,
    When they had heard these words,

  7. With Bacchus being the leader,
    With Bacchus as their leader,

°°°°°°°° Key for Chapter XX °°°°°°°°

I. A.
līberātus, -a, -um sum	cultus, -a, -um sum
līberātus, -a, -um es	cultus, -a, -um es
līberātus, -a, -um est	cultus, -a, -um est
līberātī, -ae, -a est	cultī, -ae, -a sumus
līberātī, -ae, -a estis	cultī, -ae, -a estis
līberātī, -ae, -a sunt	cultī, -ae, -a sunt

   B. he/she/it has been freed,   he/she/it has been worshipped,
        was freed   was worshipped
   C. The perfect passive participle **must agree with the noun it modifies (in this
      instance the subject of the sentence)**, which can be any gender, singular or plural.

II. 1. he is trying   6. I possessed, owned
     2. he has spoken   7. I shall possess, own
     3. we shall admire   8. they will possess, own
     4. you (s.) feared   9. he had admired
     5. you (pl.) will speak   10. we have spoken

III. 1. loquimur   7. cōnantur
     2. loquēbāmur   8. cōnābantur
     3. loquēmur   9. cōnābuntur
     4. locūtī, -ae, -a sumus   10. cōnātī, -ae, -a sunt
     5. locūtī, -ae, -a eramus 11. cōnātī, -ae, -a erant
     6. locūtī, -ae, -a erimus 12. cōnātī, -ae, -a erunt

IV. 1. Idem   6. eōdem (tempore)
     2. eandem   7. eiusdem
     3. eadem   8. eīsdem
     4. Eīdem   9. eōrundem
     5. eōdem (locō)   10. eīdem

V.   1. the state   6. of these things
     2. with faith, a pledge, trust 7. on the appointed day
     3. on/in the last days   8. the state (acc.)
     4. day and night   9. with the best hope
     5. the greatest trust (acc.)   10. things accomplished

VI. 1. We feared worse things.
     2. I (fem.) tried to leave.
     3. I suffer with you.
     4. He arose in the morning.
     5. They feared the tyrant.
     6. You (sing.) have spoken with your friends.
     7. She has spoken with her friends.
     8. The son has suffered for the sins of his father.
     9. The son ought not to suffer for the sins of his father.
     10. On each day the sun rises.

°°°°°°°° Key for Chapter XXI °°°°°°°°

I.
1. ferō	ferre	tulī	lātum	bear, carry
2. accipiō	accipere	accēpī	acceptum	receive
3. respiciō	respicere	respēxī	respectum	look back
4. inveniō	invenīre	invēnī	inventum	find, discover
5. audeō	audēre	ausus sum		dare

II.
1. bearing — pres. act. nom. sing. m.f.n., acc. sing. n.
2. (having been) received — perf. pass. nom. sing. m.
3. receiving — pres. act. nom. sing. m.f.n., acc. sing. n.
4. (having been) regained — perf. pass. nom. sing. f. or nom. or acc. pl. n.
5. (having been) discovered — perf. pass. nom. or acc. sing. m.n.
6. regaining — pres. act. nom. sing. m.f.n., acc. sing. n.
7. (having been) loved — perf. pass. nom. sing. m.
8. about to love — fut. act. nom. sing. m.
9. loving, the lovers — pres. act. nom. pl. or acc. pl., m. f.
10. carrying away — pres. act. nom. sing., m. f. n., acc. sing. n.
11. about to return — fut. act. nom. sing. m.
12. daring — pres. act. acc. sing. m.f., acc. sing. n.

III.
1. a growing boy	nom. sing.	Subj.
2. a weeping wife (or husband)	acc. sing.	Dir.Obj.
3. to him/her speaking to the man/woman as he/she spoke	dat. sing.	Ind. Obj.
4. to these departing	dat. pl.	Ind. Obj.
5. with those returning	abl. pl.	Obj. of prep. <u>cum</u>
6. him speaking	acc. sing.	Dir.Obj.
7. them speaking	acc. pl.	Dir.Obj.
8. of the singing poet	gen. sing.	Poss.
9. the god (having been) invoked	nom. sing.	Subj.
10. the songs (having been) sung	nom. or acc. pl.	Subj. or Dir.Obj.

IV.
ōmen ācre	harsh omen	ōmina ācria	harsh omens
ōminis ācris	of a harsh omen	ōminum ācrium	of harsh omens
ōminī ācrī	to/for a harsh omen	ōminibus ācribus	to/for harsh omens
ōmen ācre	harsh omen (DO)	ōmina ācria	harsh omens (DO)
ōmine ācrī	with a harsh omen	ōminibus ācribus	with harsh omens

V.
1. he has carried away
2. (having been) carried back
3. he had brought to
4. they will bear
5. they carry in
6. they will carry back
7. (having been) carried
8. he/she/it bears
9. you (pl.) have carried
10. we are bringing together

ooooooooo Key for Chapter XXII ooooooooo

I.A. vocāre — to call ⟶ vocārī — to be called
    vocāvisse — to have called ⟶ vocātus, — to have been called
    -a, -um esse
    vocātūrus, — to be about to call ⟶ vocātum īrī — to be about to be called
    -a, um esse

  B. tegere — to cover ⟶ tegī — to be covered
    texisse — to have covered ⟶ tectus, — to have been covered
    -a, um esse
    tectūrus, — to be about to cover ⟶ tectum īrī — to be about to be covered
    -a, um esse

  C. ferre — to bear ⟶ ferrī — to be borne
    tulisse — to have borne ⟶ lātus, — to have been borne
    -a, um esse
    lātūrus, — to be about to bear ⟶ lātum īrī — to be about to be borne
    -a, um esse

II. 1. to have turned out   6. to have grieved
    2. to end   7. to be about to tear to pieces
    3. to be bitten   8. to have recognized
    4. to be about to repulse   9. to be accustomed
    5. to have been covered   10. to have been carried

III. 1. a. tegere   b. tegī
     2. a. līberāre   b. līberārī
     3. a. ferre   b. ferrī
     4. a. amāre   b. amārī
     5. a. cūrāre   b. cūrārī

IV. 1. occīsūra est   2. lātūrus est   3. reflectūrus est

V. A. positive, comparative, superlative
   B. longer, more long, rather long, too long
   C. longest, most long, very long, exceedingly long
   D. 1. insānior, -ius   insānissimus, -a, -um
      2. innocentior, -ius   innocentissimus, -a, -um
      3. dīversior, -ius   dīversissimus, -a, -um
      4. melior, -ius   optimus, -a, -um
      5. maior, -ius   maximus, -a, -um

VI. 1. ventus pessimus   4. praeda maior   7. plūrimae lacrimae
    2. melius iter   5. optima causa   8. fīlia minima
    3. fīlius minor   6. fidēs maior

VII. 1. avidissimē   2. fortissimē   3. laetissimē

ANSWERS TO MUSICAL LATIN CROSSWORD PUZZLE: KEY PAGE 141

123

°°°°°°°° Key for Chapter XXIII °°°°°°°°

I. 1. venīre   2. esse   3. esse

II. 1. a. esse   2. c. mortuam esse (had died)   3. d. datūram esse

III. 1. esse   2. fuisse   3. futūram esse
     4. esse   5. fuisse   6. futūram esse

IV. 1. Quaedam   2. Quōsdam   3. quibusdam   4. quōdam   5. Quōrundam
    6. quōdam   7. quendam   8. cuidam   9. cuiusdam   10. Quaedam

V. solus   sōla   sōlum   sōlī   sōlae   sōla
    sōlīus   sōlīus   sōlīus   sōlōrum   sōlārum   sōlōrum
    sōlī   sōlī   sōlī   sōlīs   sōlīs   sōlīs
    sōlum   sōlam   sōlum   sōlōs   sōlās   sōla
    sōlō   sōlā   sōlō   sōlīs   sōlīs   sōlīs

ūnus, nullus, ullus, sōlus, neuter, alter, uter, tōtus, alius
ūnus nauta

°°°°°°°° Key for Chapter XXIV °°°°°°°°°
I. B.
 1. Vocēmus   call   10. Pōnātur   be placed or put
 2. Doceat   teach   11. Committās   bring together
 3. Dūcās   lead   12. Concipiam   undertake
 4. Capiam   take   13. Concurrant   run together
 5. Audiant   hear   14. Exhortēmur   urge
 6. Existimētis   think   15. Fatear   confess
 7. Stet   stand   16. Gravēris   be weighed down
 8. Sequāminī   follow   17. Nē metuāmus   let us not fear
 9. Arbitrēmur   think   18. Nē nāvigēmus   let us not sail

II. sim   sīmus   possim   possīmus
    sīs   sītis   possīs   possītis
    sit   sint   possit   possint

III. 1. per aquam   6. ā saxīs
     2. in aquam   7. ad saxa
     3. circum saxum   8. ex aquā
     4. in aquā   9. inter piscēs
     5. trans aquam   10. sub saxum or saxō (depending on verb)

IV. 1. sim   2. possint   3. sim   4. sīs
    5. possītis   6. sit   7. sīmus   8. possint

V. 1. j. melior   6. d. falsus
   2. g. honestus   7. h. grātus
   3. i. longus   8. e. benignus
   4. b. multī   9. a. in perīculō
   5. f. maior   10. c. miser

VI. A. Against Jason: 1. Occidat!   For Jason: 1. Vīvat!
                     2. trādam   2. amem
                     3. sit   3. sit
                     4. det   4. sint
                     5. relinquamne   5. noscam

   B.   trādam   capiam   veniam
        trādam   capiam   veniam
   The only way to tell the difference is by context, since the forms are identical.

VII. 1. i. corpus   6. d. caelum
     2. e. virtus or fortitūdo (courage) 7. j. fīlius or nātus
     3. a. frāter   8. g. arātrum
     4. c. amor or commōtio (emotion) 9. h. initium
     5. f. mens sāna   10. b. nox

°°°°°°°° Key for Chapter XXV °°°°°°°°

I. infintive + personal endings, both active and passive

II. 1. nāvigāret   6. caderēs
    2. manērent   7. ardērentur
    3. mitterem   8. disceret
    4. facerētur   9. converterēmur
    5. sentīrētis   10. effugerem

III. Purpose clauses:
     1. reciperet: Medea went into the forest to obtain her magic herbs.
     2. dūceret: Jason promised to marry Medea. (to lead into marriage)
     3. daret: Jason promised marriage so that Medea might give him aid.
     4. coleret: Jason placed the yoke on the bulls to plow the field.
     5. converteret: Jason threw a rock among the men to turn the struggle from himself.
     6. ageret: Medea sang songs (did her singing) to thank the gods.
     7. potīrētur: Jason had come to get possession of the golden fleece.

IV. Result clauses:
    1. habēret: The woman had so many children that she did not have enough food.
    2. daret: Medea had such great love that she gave aid to Jason.
    3. timēret: Aeetes gave so many labors to Jason that the hero feared greatly
                     (was very afraid).
    4. amāret: Jason was so handsome that Medea loved him immediately.
    5. posset: The dragon was so horrible that no one could get possession
                     of the golden fleece.

V. 1. so that he might follow   6. fatērētur
   2. so that we might try   7. arbitrārentur
   3. so that you (pl.) might urge   8. nascerēris
   4. so that they might get possession of 9. morīrēminī
   5. so that I might be born   10. ēgrederer

ETYMOLOGY GAMES

I.			II.		
3.	a.		9.	a.	
6.	b.		11.	b.	
10.	c.		13.	c.	
2.	d.		7.	d.	
7.	e.		12.	e.	
9.	f.		2.	f.	
5.	g.		8.	g.	
4.	h.		4.	h.	
1.	i.		3.	i.	
8.	j.		10.	j.	
			6.	k.	
			5.	l.	
			1.	m.	

°°°°°°°° Key for Chapter XXVI °°°°°°°°

I. Active: perfect stem + future of <u>sum</u> (written as one word)
   Passive: perfect passive participle + present subjunctive of <u>sum</u> (written as two words)

II. 1. perf. 3rd sing. act.   3. perf. 1st pl. act
    2. perf. 2nd pl. act.   4. perf. 3rd sing. pass.

III. Active: perfect infinitive + personal endings (written as one word)
     Passive: perfect passive participle + imperfect subjunctive of <u>sum</u> (written as two words)
          vocātus esset   doctus esset   missus esset   factus esset   sēnsus esset

IV. 1. pluperf. 1st sing. act.
    2. pluperf. 3rd pl. act.
    3. pluperf. 3rd sing. deponent verb; pass. forms, act. meaning
    4. pluperf. 1st sing. act.

V.

1.	a.	<u>avis</u>, bird
7.	b.	<u>arbor</u>, tree
10.	c.	<u>sacerdōs</u>, priest
5.	d.	<u>gladiator</u>
4.	e.	<u>Circus Maximus</u>, Circus Maximus
9.	f.	<u>mānēs</u>, shades of the dead
8.	g.	<u>agnus</u>, lamb
12.	h.	<u>pōmum pressum</u>, pressed apple
11	i.	<u>gallīna</u>, chicken
6.	j.	<u>vacca</u>, cow
3.	k.	<u>senex</u>, old man
2	l.	<u>coquus</u>, cook

VI. 1. amāret ... dūceret
    2. amāvisset ... relīquisset
    3. posset ... mūtāret
    4. potuisset ... mūtāvisset
    5. secūtus esset ... occīdisset

VII. A. Indirect Object

B. A compound verb is one that is composed of a main verb stem
prefixed by another word, usually a preposition.

C. 1. Mihi ... Minervae   4. illīs   7. Fīliō
    2. Tibi   5. Mīlitibus   8. exercituī
    3. mihi   6. Theseō   9. vōbīs

°°°°°°° Key for Chapter XXVII °°°°°°°

I. A. Indicative: 6   Subjunctive: 4
    Present   Perfect   Present   Perfect
    Imperfect Pluperfect   Imperfect   Pluperfect
    Future   Future Perfect
There are no future tenses in the subjunctive because the whole idea of the
subjunctive is in the realm of futurity, unreality, possibility, or probability.
    B. Active: mittat   mīserit   Passive: mittātur   missus sit
               mitteret   mīsisset   mitterētur   missus esset

II. 1. Quis   3. Cūr   5. Quō locō/Ubi   7. Quōmodo
    2. Quid   4. Ubi/Quō locō 6. Quandō

III. 1. sīs   1. He knows who you are.
     2. faciat   2. He knows what she is doing.
     3. veniat   3. He knows why she is coming.
     4. exerceant   4. He knows where they are training.
     5. sit   5. He knows where the Isthmus is.
     6. sit   6. He knows when the race is.
     7. vincat   7. He knows how Theseus wins.

IV. 1. quis essēs.   1. He knew who you were.
    2. quid faceret.   2. He knew what she did.
    3. cūr venīret.   3. He knew why she came.
    4. ubi exercērent.   4. He knew where they were training.
    5. quō locō Isthmus esset. 5. He knew where the Isthmus was.
    6. quandō certāmen esset.   6. He knew when the race was.
    7. quōmodo Thēseus vinceret. 7. He knew how Theseus won.

V. 1. Scīvit quis fuissēs.   1. He knew who you had been.
   2. Scīvit quid fēcisset.   2. He knew what she had done.
   3. Scīvit cūr vēnisset.   3. He knew why she had come.
   4. Scīvit ubi exercuissent.   4. He knew where they had trained.
   5. Scīvit quō locō Isthmus fuisset 5. He knew where the Isthmus had been.
   6. Scīvit quandō certāmen fuisset. 6. He knew when the race had been.
   7. Scīvit quōmodo Thēseus vīcisset. 7. He knew how Theseus had won.

VI. locō, locāre, locāvī, locātum meaning to put or to place
    1. Rōmam   3. Athēnīs   5. ad Āfricam   7. domī
    2. Rōmae   4. in Siciliā 6. in Āfricā   8. rūrī

Church Latin: ANSWERS TO CROSSWORD PUZZLE: KEY, PAGE 142

°°°°°°° Key for Chapter XXVIII °°°°°°°

I. A. A preposition meaning "with," or a subordinate conjunction,
   meaning "when, since, because, or although."

B.
1. Prep.	with		6. Sub. Conj.	when, since, because
2. Prep.	with		7. Sub. Conj.	when
3. Sub. Conj.	when		8. Sub. Conj.	when
4. Prep.	with		9. Prep.	with
5. Sub. Conj.	when		10. Sub. Conj.	when, since, because

II. 1. When Theseus took the cup from the king, Aegeus recognized the ornament
       of the sword.
   2. Because his son had been found, the king greatly rejoiced.
   3. When Medea saw that her crime was disclosed, she was greatly afraid
       and wished to leave.
   4. Although the isthmus had been calmed, nevertheless the citizens feared
       the white bull.
   5. Because Androgeus had been killed, Minos ordered that seven youths and
       seven maidens be sent to Crete.
   6. When the two-formed monster had been born to Pasiphae, Minos tried to
       hide the offspring under the palace.
   7. Although the seven youths and maidens had been chosen by lot, nevertheless
       Theseus determined also to go with them.
   8. Since these things are so, a most miserable Aegeus sees that his son is departing.
   9. When there was peace in the city, the men could work more easily.

III. 1. patrī   2. Mēdēae   3. parentī

IV.
Comparative	Superlative
1. longior, -ius	longissimus, -a, -um
2. facilior, -ius	facillimus, -a, -um
3. difficilior, -ius	difficillimus, -a, -um
4. miserior, -ius	miserrimus, -a, -um
5. sacrior, -ius	sacerrimus, -a, -um
6. ācrior, -ius	ācerrimus, -a, -um
7. melior, -ius	optimus, -a, -um
8. peior, -ius	pessimus, -a, -um
9. minor, minus	minimus, -a, -um
10. maior, maius	maximus, -a, -um
11. _____, plūs	plūrimus, -a, -um

V. 1. Optimus (homo)   3. difficillimum ... optimum   5. sacerrimum   7. clarior
   2. facillimum ... pessimum 4. optima or optimae res   6. pēiorēs

°°°°°°°° Key for Chapter XXIX °°°°°°°°°

I.
quī	quae	quod	who, what	quī	quae	quae
cuius	cuius	cuius	whose, of whom	quōrum	quārum	quōrum
cui	cui	cui	to/for whom,	quibus	quibus	quibus
quem	quam	quod	whom, that, which	quōs	quās	quae
quō	quā	quō	by whom, which	quibus	quibus	quibus

128

II. This noun is called the <u>antecedent</u>. The relative pronoun must agree with this noun in <u>gender</u> and <u>number</u>, but it takes its case from its use in its own clause.

1. b. quae	4. d. cui	7. a. quod	10. b. quōs
2. c. quod	5. b. quō	8. c. quem	11. c. quam
3. a. quī	6. c. quī	9. d. cuius	

III. <u>Antecedent</u>   <u>Relative Pronoun</u>

1. <u>Pasiphae</u>	Fem. Sing	quae	Nom. Subj.
2. <u>monstrum</u>	Neut. Sing.	quod	Acc. Dir. Obj.
3. <u>Minos</u>	Masc. Sing.	quī	Nom. Subj.
4. <u>Daedalus</u>	Masc. Sing.	cui	Dat. Ind. Obj.
5. <u>labyrinthum</u>	Masc. Sing.	quō	Abl. Obj. Prep.
6. <u>Iuvenes</u>	Masc. Pl.	quī	Nom. Subj.
7. <u>velo</u>	Neut. Sing.	quod	Nom. Subj.
8. <u>anulum</u>	Masc. Sing.	quem	Acc. Dir. Obj.
9. <u>Ariadna</u>	Fem. Sing.	cuius	Gen. Poss.
10. <u>Iuvenes</u>	Masc. Pl.	quōs	Acc. Dir. Obj.
11. <u>Ariadna</u>	Fem. Sing.	quam	Acc. Dir. Obj.

IV. 1. Minos was the kind of king who would conceal the Minotaur.
2. Theseus was the sort of hero who would kill the Minotaur.
3. Aegeus was the kind of parent who would kill himself if his son had been killed.
4. Theseus loved the kind of woman who would give him help.
5. Theseus showed the youths the sort of string by means of which they might escape.

V. 1. It is permitted for you to smoke in this place.
Smoking is permitted here. or You may smoke here.
2. It is pleasing for students to read books.
Students like to read books.
3. It is necessary for students to study, if they want to learn.
Students have to study, if they want to learn.
4. It pleases me to write this letter to you.
I am glad to be writing this letter to you.
5. It is necessary to have friends, if you wish to be happy.
You must have friends, if you want to be happy.
6. It is permitted for you to play after work.
You may play after work.
7. To no one is it ever permitted to know (It is not permitted that anyone ever know) what he did.
No one should ever know what he did.

VI. A. verbal noun
B. Sing. only: Gen., Dat., Acc., Abl.
C. the infinitive
D. <u>-ndī</u>   E. of building

F. 1. the love of learning
    2. the hope of escaping
    3. the skill of healing
    4. the art of deceiving
    5. the love of running
    6. the love of building
    7. the art of constructing
    8. the art of teaching
    9. the opportunity of conquering
    10. a time of/for being born
    11. a time of/for dying

G. 1. Discipulus amōrem discendī habet.
    2. Servī spem effugiendī habent.
    3. Medicī facultātem sānandī habent.
    4. Magī artem dēcipiendī habent.
    5. Cursōrēs amōrem currendī habent.
    6. Architectī amōrem aedificandī habent.
    7. Structōrēs artem construendī habent.
    8. Magister artem docendī habet.
    9. Imperātor opportūnitātem vincendī habet.
    10. Omnēs tempus nascendī habent.
    11. Hērōs tempus moriendī habet.

°°°°°°°° Key for Chapter XXX °°°°°°°°

I. A. volō, velle, voluī

B. volo
   vīs
   vult
   volumus
   vultis
   volunt

C. vult
   volēbat
   volet
   voluit
   voluerat
   voluerint

   velit
   vellet

   voluerit
   voluisset

   D. 1. nōn vīs   nōn vultis   2. nōn vult   3. mālumus

II. A. nōlī   nōlīte
    B. to introduce a negative command
    C. 1. Nōlī cogere ....
       2. Nōlīte commovēre!
       3. Nōlī implōrāre.
       4. nōlīte meī oblīviscī
       5. nōlī respondere
    D. 1. I did not want to disturb the citizens.
       2. We preferred to forget the battle.
       3. He did not want to be considered an emperor.
       4. Let them prefer good things, not bad ones.
       5. If his wife had not wanted very costly gifts, her husband
       would not have left her.

III. 1. daret
     2. ornāret
     3. occīderent
     4. hūmāret
     5. iuvāret

IV. 1. adiuvārent
    2. māllēs
    3. esset
    4. amāret
    5. mīrārētur

Legal Latin: ANSWERS TO CROSSWORD PUZZLE: KEY, PAGE 143

°°°°°°° Key for Chapter XXXI °°°°°°°

I. A. dactylic hexameter
   B. dactyl: long, short, short   spondee: long, long
   C. six feet to a verse (to each line of poetry)
   D. 1. if it contains a long vowel
      2. if it contains a diphthong
      3. if it contains a short vowel followed by two consonants
   E. Elision is the sliding together of two vowels, one ending a word and the other
      beginning a word. It also occurs when a word ends in -m followed by a word
      beginning with a vowel or h..
   F. Caesura is the natural pause in a line within a foot when a word ends, usually in the
      third or fourth foot.

   G. atque in|rēgĕ tămen păter|est;‖ĕgŏ|mītĕ părentis

      ingĕnĭum verbīs‖ad| publĭcă|commŏdă|vertī:

      difficĭllem tĕnuī‖sŭb ĭnīquō|iudĭce|causam.

      Hunc tămĕn|utĭlĭtās‖pŏpŭlī frătĕrque dătīque

      summă mŏvet scepĕrī,‖laudem ŭt cum| sanguĭnĕ|penset;

II. 1. vīdērunt, _they have seen_   3. mūtāvisse, _to have changed_
    2. parāvissent, _they would have prepared_   4. futūrm esse, _to be going to be,_
                                                      about to be

III. fīō   fīs   fit   fīmus   fītis   fīunt
     eō   īs   it   īmus   ītis   eunt

IV. fit   fīat   it   eat
     fīēbat   fieret   ībat   īret
     fīet   ībit
     factus est   factus sit   īvit   īverit
     factus erat factus esset īverat īvisset
     factus erit   īverit

V. 1. Paris never became a great hero.
   2. Neptune became violent on the waves.
   3. Agamemnon was made leader of the Greeks.
   4. With Aegeus dead, Theseus became king at Athens.
   5. Iphigenia was made (or became) a sacrifice to the virgin goddess.
   6. Let there be light, and there was light.

VI. 1. If Paris gives (lit. will have given) the golden apple to Venus, the goddess
       will give him the most beautiful woman.
    2. If Paris goes (lit. will go) to Sparta, he himself will see Helen.
    3. If Paris sees (lit. will have seen) Helen, he will desire her.

4. If Paris desires (lit. will desire) Helen, he will carry her off.

5. If Paris carries off (lit. will have carried off) Helen, there will be war between the Greeks and the Trojans.

Future or Future Perfect of the Indicative Mood.

VII. 1. raperet, ... esset
rapuisset, ... fuisset
If Paris had not carried off Helen, there would not have been war.

2. If savage winds at Aulis were not making the sea impassable, the Greeks would be sailing to Troy.
fēcissent, ... nāvigāvissent
If savage winds at Aulis had not made the sea impassable, the Greeks would have sailed to Troy.

3. If Ajax were going to Clytemnestra, the mother would not be sending Iphigenia.
īvisset, ... mīsisset
If Ajax had gone to Clytemnestra, the mother would not have sent Iphigenia.

4. If Agamemnon were not sacrificing his daughter, Diana would not be changing the winds.
sacrificāvisset, ... mūtāvisset
If Agamemnon had not sacrificed his daughter, Diana would not have changed the winds.

5. If you were not studying the Latin language, you would not be reading this story.
studuissētis, ... lēgissētis
If you had not studied the Latin language, you would not have read this story.

VIII. 1. reveniat ... necet
2. reveniat ... ignoscat

IX. A. 1. Mars
2. Aperīre or Aphrodite
3. Maia or Maiōres (the elders)
4. Jūno or Jūniōres (the younger ones)
5. Julius Caesar, originally Quintilis, the 5th month
6. Caesar Augustus , originally Sextilis, the 6th month
7. septem, the 7th month
8. octō, the 8th month
9. novem, the 9th month
10. decem, the 10th month

B. 1. Janus   Janus was the two-headed god who faced in two directions, the god of beginning and ending.
2. Februae   days of atonement

C. 1. Kalendae, the first of the month
2. Nōnes,   the seventh or the fifth
3. Ides,   the fifteenth or the thirteenth

132

D. In March, July, October, May,
   The Ides come on the fifteenth day,
   The Nones the seventh, and all besides,
   Have two days less for Nones and Ides.

E. January 1   May 7   March 15
   the murder of Julius Caesar

°°°°°°°°° Key for Chapter XXXII °°°°°°°°°

I. cōnātur   cōnētur   sequuntur   sequantur
    cōnābātur cōnārētur   sequēbantur sequerentur
    cōnābitur   sequentur
    cōnātus est cōnātus sit   secūtī sunt secūtī sint
    cōnātus erat cōnātus esset secūtī erant secūtī essent
    cōnātus erit   secūtī erunt

II. cōnāns   sequēns
           cōnātus   secūtus
   cōnātūrus cōnandus   secūtūrus   sequendus

III. cōnārī   sequī
    cōnātus esse   secūtus esse
    cōnātūrus esse   secūtūrus esse

IV. 1. mīrāre   mīrāminī
    2. tuēre   tuēminī
    3. ēgredere   ēgrediminī
    4. potīre   potīminī
    5. orīre   orīminī
    6. nascere   nasciminī

V. 1. Quis est Helena?
   2. Ubi Helena habitat?
   3. Cūr Helena cum eō īre dēbet?
   4. Quōmodō Helenam rapere dēbet?

   1. Paris scit quis Helena sit.
   2. Paris scit ubi Helena habitet.
   3. Paris scit cūr Helena cum eō īre dēbeat.
   4. Paris scit quōmodō Helenam rapere dēbeat.

VI. 1. Graecī rogāvērunt quis rēx esset.
    2. Graecī rogāvērunt ubi bellum esset.
    3. Graecī rogāvērunt cūr pugnāre **dēbērent**. (Note subject change)
    4. Graecī rogāvērunt quōmodō Ulixēs nāvigāret.

°°°°°° Chapter for Chapter XXXIII °°°°°°°

I. A.

is	ea	id		eī	eae	ea
eius	eius	eius		eōrum	eārum	eōrum
eī	eī	eī		eīs	eīs	eīs
eum	eam	id		eōs	eās	ea
eō	eā	eō		eīs	eīs	eīs

B. Every final -m would become -n before -dem, and Nom. Masc. Sing. <u>Idem.</u>

C. <u>Genitive</u> singular, ending in <u>-ius</u>; <u>dative</u> singular in <u>-ī</u>.

II.

1. this man, that man, the same man, the man himself, that fellow
2. to this woman, to that woman, to the same woman, to the woman herself, to that woman
3. These, Those, The same, The birds themselves, Those birds
4. This one, That one, The same one, the animal itself, that one (that beast)
5. These, Those, The same, The bodies themselves, Those

III. A. licet, licēre, licuit
   B. Licet vōbīs (in) librum inspicere.
   C. viz = <u>videlicet</u>, you may see, namely, that is to say
   D. sc = <u>scilicet</u>, you may know, namely, that is to say

IV.
1. Ulysses is wiser than Ajax, isn't he?	(Yes)
2. Helen is immortal, isn't she?	(Yes)
3. Ajax was not wise, was he?	(No)
4. Ajax was stronger than Ulysses, wasn't he?	(Yes)
5. Ajax was not sent as a brave orator to the citadel, was he?	(No)
6. Ajax did not demand the return of Helen, did he?	(No)
7. Ulysses was a better orator than Ajax, wasn't he?	(Yes)

V. 1. praedae
   2. honōris
   3. mortis
   4. bonae fortūnae
   5. hominum

VI. 1. domum 2. rūs 3. Ulixem 4. decem annōs

ᵒᵒᵒᵒᵒᵒ Key for Chapter XXXIV ᵒᵒᵒᵒᵒᵒᵒ

I. A. three   B. praenomen   nomen   cognomen
   C. -puer attached to the name of the master: Marcipor, Marcus's boy
   D. the female equivalent of the father's name: Tullius > Tullia

   E. Leo: lion   Rex: king   Dexter: right handed, skillful
      Alma: kind   Clara: bright   Lucy: full of light

II. vocāns   calling

                                          vocātus, -a, -um   (having been) called
      vocātūrus, -a, -um   (about) to call   vocandus, -a, -um   (about) to be called

      mittēns   sending

                                          missus, -a, -um   (having been) sent
      missūrus, -a , -um   (about) to send   mittendus, -a, -um   (about) to be sent

   present active
   perfect passive
   future active
   future passive, also called the gerundive

III. A. verbal adjective   B. verbal noun

    C. 1. The cook was thinking about preparing the dinner. (lit. the
           dinner that was about to be prepared)
       2. Polyxena, about to be killed, was snatched from her
           mother's bosom.
       3. Hecuba wept for her daughter (who was) about to be killed.
       4. The women about to be carried off kissed (gave kisses to)
           the Trojan earth.
       5. I am thinking about the letter (that is) about to be written.
           I am thinking about writing the letter.

IV. A. roundabout, a roundabout way of speaking, circumlocution
    B. The island ought to be seen from a distance. (Obligation or necessity is implied;
        in other words, you ought to see this island from a distance; you ought to stay
        away. It is dangerous to see this island up close; stay away from this island.)
    C. 1. Amīcī vōbīs monendī sunt.
       2. Linguae nōbīs discendae sunt.
       3. Parentēs eī parendī sunt.
       4. Patria tibi servanda est.
       5. Canēs līberīs cūrandī sunt.
       6. Cibus mātribus parandus est.
       7. Malī (virī) nōbīs timendī sunt.
       8. Līberī videndī nōn audiendī sunt.
       9. Animālia nōbīs amanda sunt.
      10. Fīliī patrī suō amandī sunt.

135

°°°°°° Key for Chapter XXXV °°°°°°°

I. fert   fertur   ferat   ferātur
    ferēbat   ferēbātur   ferret   ferrētur
    feret   ferētur
    tulit   lātus est   tulerit   lātus sit
    tulerat   lātus erat   tulisset   lātus esset
    tulerit   lātus erit

    Participles: Pres.Act. ferēns
                                          Perf. Pass. lātus, -a, -um
                  Fut. Act. lātūrus, -a, -um   Fut. Pass. ferendus, -a, -um

    Imperatives: Fer! Ferte! Infinitives: ferre   ferrī
                                           tulisse   lātus esse
                                           lātūrus esse   lātum īrī

II. est   sit   potest   possit
    erat   esset   poterat   posset
    erit   poterit
    fuit   fuerit   potuit   potuerit
    fuerat   fuisset   potuerat   potuisset
    fuerit   potuerit

    esse   posse
    fuisse   potuisse
    futūrus esse

III. A. 1. Let us praise brave men!
        2. What am I to do? What can I say?
        3. Would that my mother were alive!
        4. No one can say that I am unhappy.

    B. 1. The artist paints the vases with colors to tell his stories. (so that
             he may tell his stories)
       2. Polyphemus was so cruel that he devoured men.
       3. a. If the sailors should open the sack of winds, the winds would escape.
          b. If the sailors had not opened the sack of winds, the winds would not
               have escaped.
       4. a. When the Laestrygonians sank the rest of the ships, Ulysses' ship alone escaped.
          b. Because the ship was approaching the Sirens, Ulysses sealed the ears
               of his men with wax.
          c. Although the Scylla was now a monster, nevertheless she had once been
               a beautiful maiden.
       5. Circe asked Ulysses to remain with her.
          Ulysses persuaded Circe to turn back his men, now swine, into human beings.
       6. Penelope wondered who the stranger was.
          Ulysses knew who the suitors were and what they were doing.

7. a. Penelope was not the sort of wife who would be unfaithful.
   b. The suitors sent servants to invite Penelope to the banquet.
8. a. Penelope feared that Ulysses would not come home.
   b. Penelope feared lest she be led ito marriage by a suitor.
9. a. Ulysses knew that the suitors who lived in the were evil.
   b. Ulysses asked his son to help him kill the suitors who were in
      the palace.
10. a. He waited until the rest of the ships arrived (might arrive).
    b. The Greeks waited until fair winds moved (would move) the ships.

ᵒᵒᵒᵒᵒᵒ Key for Chapter XXXVI ᵒᵒᵒᵒᵒᵒᵒ

I. 1. redūceret
   Aeneas sent his companion to bring (lit. to lead) Ascanius.
  2. invenīrent
   Dido sent messengers to find Aeneas.

II.   1. Laokoon ran down to warn the Trojans.
III. 1. Laokoon ran down to warn the Trojans.
IV.   1. Laokoon ran down to warn the Trojans.
V.   1. Laokoon ran down for the sake of warning the Trojans.
      2. Laokoon ran down for the sake of warning the Trojans.
VI.   Laokoon sent his sons to warn (who might warn) the Trojans.

VII. A.
Purpose Clause: Aenēas socium mīsit ut Ascanium redūceret.
Supine: Aenēas socium mīsit Ascanium reductum.
Ad + Gerund: Aenēas socium mīsit ad Ascanium redūcendum.
Ad + Gerundive: Aenēas socium mīsit ad Ascanium redūcendum.
These two look similar in ending because the gerundive is modifying a masculine
accusative singular, Ascanium, which has the same case ending as the gerund.
  Causā + Gerundive: Aenēas socium mīsit Ascaniī redūcendī causā.
  Grātiā + Gerund: Aenēas socium mīsit Ascanium redūcendī grātiā.
   (N.B.: with an object, better Latin uses the **gerundive**, as above)
  Relative Clause: Aenēas mīsit socium quī Ascanium redūceret.

  B.
Purpose Clause: Dīdō nuntiōs mīsit ut Aenēan invenīrent.
Supine: Dīdō nuntiōs mīsit Aenēan inventum.
Ad + Gerund: Dīdō nuntiōs mīsit ad Aenēan inveniendum.
Ad + Gerundive: Dīdō nuntiōs mīsit ad Aenēan inveniendum.
These two look the similar because the gerundive is modifying Aenēan, the Greek masculine
accusative singular, same case as the gerund, although the Greek accusative ends in -an.
  Causā + Gerundive: Dīdō nuntiōs mīsit Aenēae inveniendī causā.
  Grātiā + Gerund: Dīdō nuntiōs mīsit Aenēan inveniendī grātiā.
   (N.B.: with an object, better Latin uses the **gerundive**, as above)
  Relative Clause: Dīdō mīsit nuntiōs quī Aenēan invenīrent.

VIII. 1. ientaculum   2. prandium   3. cēna

°°°°°° Key for Chapter XXXVII °°°°°°°

I. 1. c) sagittā   6. d) vītā   quam vīta (est) is also possible
   2. a) cum fīliō   7. a) illīs   quam illī (sunt) is also possible
   3. b) ā Trōiānō   8. c) magnā cum cūrā
   4. a) vī   9. d) Italicō profundō
   5. c) tābō   10. c) in silvā

II. 1.a) in īnsulā minōre quam Sicilia (est).   6. c) moritūrī
       c) in īnsulā minōre Siciliā.   7. b) petentibus
    2. b) benignius   8. a) exercitū victō
    3. b) ortus est or oriēbātur   9. c) bene doctī
    4. c) ludentēs
    5. b) patī

            10. a) Nōs omnēs patriam amāre dēbēmus.
                c) Patria nōbīs omnibus amanda est.
            11. d) Carthāgō dēlenda est. or
   Cato could also have said: c) Carthāginem dēlēre dēbēmus.

°°°°°° Key for Chapter XXXVIII °°°°°°°

I. A. 1. vestibulum   6. impluvium
      2. atrium   7. tablīnum
      3. cubicula   8. triclinium
      4. alae   9. latrīna
      5. compluvium   10. culīna
                         11. peristylum

   B. 1. īnsula
      2. Because it rises like an island from the "sea" of
         streets around it.

II. 1. Bonōrum amīcōrum   3. omnium   5. deōrum
    2. diēī nātālis   4. vestimentōrum

III. 1.The doctor studies the art of healing.   Gerund
     2. We have devoted ourselves to visiting Greece.   Gerundive
     3. Poets are skilled in the art of wrriting.   Gerund
     4. You devoted yourself to learning music.   Gerundive
     5. My daughter devoted herself to teaching.   Gerund
     6. Your son devoted himself to seeking good fortune. Gerundive
     7. You will learn to swim by swimming.   Gerund

IV. 7. Polyphemus   2. Circe
     9. Nereids   4. Elpenor
     3. Mercury   5. Eurylochus
     1. Antiphates   8. Laestrygonians
    10. Ulysses   6. Achaemenides

°°°°°° Key for Chapter XXXIX °°°°°°°

I. It has "laid aside" its active forms and although it looks
   passive, it must be translated as active.

II. 6 tenses: Pres, Imp, Fut, Perf. Past Perf., Fut Perf. (same as
       for a regular verb)

III. 4 moods: Indicative, Subjunctive, Imperative, Infinitive

IV. A. I   II   III   III -iō   IV
        a   ē   i   i   ī
    B. e   ea   a   ia   ia
            (same as for a regular verb)

V. Infinitive (a reconstructed active infinitive) + passive endings
       (same as for a regular verb)

VI. 4   cōnāns   sequēns
        cōnātus   secūtus
        cōnātūrus   secūtūrus
        cōnandus   sequendus

VII. 3 cōnārī   sequī
        cōnātus esse   secūtus esse
        cōnātūrus esse   secūtūrus esse

VIII.   cōnāre   cōnāminī   sequere   sequiminī

IX.   cōnāris(re) cōnēris(re)   sequiminī   sequāminī
      cōnābāris   cōnārēris   sequēbāminī sequerēminī
      cōnāberis   sequēminī

      cōnātus es   cōnātus sīs   secūtī estis   secūtī sītis
      cōnātus erās cōnātus essēs secūtī erātis secūtī essētis
      cōnātus eris   secūtī eritis

X. 1. they fear   6. he/she/it would/might follow
   2. they were speaking   7. wondering
   3. you will obtain   8. about to speak
   4. I wondered (lady speaking) 9. If I were obtaining
   5. Let him/her/it follow   10. If I had obtained

XI. 1. Ō, Trōiāne   7. mī fīlī
    2. coniūnx or uxor   8. meae fīliae
    3. sacerdōtēs   9. Ō, parentēs
    4. Ō, optime vir or hērōs 10. meī līberī
       Ō, maxime vir or hērōs 11. mī amīce
    5. māter   12. līberī
    6. Ō, dī (deī)   13. Piger

°°°°°° Key for Chapter XL °°°°°°°

I. 1. multīs deīs
   2. līberīs (suīs)
   3. mīlitibus (suīs)
   4. amīcīs (vestrīs)
   5. parentibus (vestrīs)
   6. ferulae
   7. discipulīs (suīs)
   8. magistrō (suō) / magistrae (suae)
   9. bonō dominō
   10. artī
   11. Mihi

II. 1. Eī crēdam.
   2. Ignosce mihi, pater.
   3. Nōlīte eīs nocēre!
   4. Parce fēminīs!
   5. Parē iūdicibus.
   6. Iūdicī persuādēbit.
   7. Rēgī placent.
   8. Nullī dominō serviō.
   9. Novīs (rēbus) studēmus.
   10. Imperā mihi et parēbō.

III. A. 1. fīliō
    2. parentibus

   B. 1. suō patrī Iovī
    2. suae mātrī
    3. animālibus

   C. 1. mīlitibus
    2. tibi

   D. 1. Turnō (Dat. of Agent)
    2. Trōiānō Aenēae (Dat. of Agent)

   E. 1. tibi
    2. Mihi

   F. 1. auxiliō hērōī

   G. 1. mīlitibus (Dat. of Compound)

Word List: Partes Corporis

auris	digitus	pes
capilli	lingua	talus
clavicula	membrum	tibia
collus	musculus	truncus
corpus	nasus	vertebra
crus	oculus	venter
cutis	os	
dentes	pectus	

Answers: Partes Corporis (Body Parts) Crossword Puzzle

```
        C   MUSCULUS  P
        R   T     O   I     E
      CUTIS   L   NASUS   M
        S  B   C L   G       E
        I    O U   U         M
          AURIS    A         B
        V      P             R
        PECTUS      TRUNCUS
          N            A     M
      DIGITUS   CAPILLI
      E     E          U
      N VERTEBRA  OS
      T       R       C
      E       U       U
      S       N       L
          CLAVICULA
          U       S
          S
```

Word List: Musical Latin

allegro	fugue	rhythm
alto	harmony	septet
cadence	lento	sextet
clef	octet	solo
conespressomolto	pianissimo	soprano
crescendo	piano	tempo
duet	plectrum	trio
forte	quartet	vivace
fortissimo	quintet	

Answers: Musical Crossword Puzzle

```
        V       F
        I       U           H A R M O N Y
        V       G           L
        A       U           T
C   C   C R E S C E N D O
A L L E G R O               U
D       N       F   E       P
E   S E P T E T     F O R T I S S I M O
N       S       R       E   A       C
C L E F     P   L E N T O   X   N   T
E       T   R       E       T   O   E
        R   S   S   Q       E       T
  P I A N I S S I M O   Q U A R T E T
        O   S   L   I
            O   O   N
  R H Y T H M       T
            O   P L E C T R U M
            L           T
        T E M P O
S O P R A N O
```

Word List: Church Latin

advent	communion	credo
altar	confession	genesis
angel	confirmation	testament
ascension	congregation	vespers
beatitudes	convent	vestment
benediction	conversion	
commandment	creation	

Answers: Church Latin Crossward Puzzle

```
A D V E N T             B
S                       E           G
C O N F I R M A T I O N E
E                       D       C O N V E N T
N                       O       E
S               C O M M U N I O N       S
I               C       G       I           C
O           A       A L T A R   S           O
N       C   N       N           I           N
        O   G       O       G       C       F
    C O N V E R S I O N       A       R     E
  C     G   L               T       E     S
  R     R       B E A T I T U D E S
V E S P E R S           O       O       I
A       G       V E S T M E N T         O
T       A               N
I       T E S T A M E N T
O       I
N   C O M M A N D M E N T
    N
```

Word List: Legal Latin

amicus curiae	inter vivos	res ipsa loquitur
causa mortis	nolo contendere	stirpes
ex parte	nunc pro tunc	sua sponte
habeas corpus	pari passu	sub poena
in rem	prima facie	ultra vires

Answers: Legal Latin Crossword Puzzle

```
                                        P
                                        A
                                        R               I N R E M
                          H             I
                  E X P A R T E         N I
                          B             T P
          N O L O C O N T E N D E R E   A S
                  A       A         U   V S
          P       U       S         L   I U
      S   R       S       C         T   V
      U   I       A       O         R   O
      B   M       M       R         A   S
      P   A       O       P         V
      O   F       R       U         I
      E   A       T       S   T I R P E S
      N   C       I           R
      A M I C U S C U R I A E R
          E       T       U   E
                  N           S U A S P O N T E
                  C
```

```
                    P
                    A
                    R                 I N R E M
              H     I
        E X P A R T E                 N   I                M
              B                       T   P                R
    N O L O C O N T E N D E R E       E   A                E
              A       A         U     R   S                S
      P       U       S         L     V   S                I
  S   R       S       C         T     I   U                P
  U   I       A       O         R     V                    S
  B   M       M       R         A     O                    A
  P   A       O       P         V     S                    L
  O   F       R       U                                    O
  E   A       T       S       T I R P E S                  Q
  N   C       I                     R                      U
  A M I C U S C U R I A E           E                      I
      E       T                     S U A S P O N T E      T
              N                                            U
              C                                            R
```